The information and content contained in this publication are from the experiences and views of the Author and does not necessarily represent the views of any organization or person.

First Edition

Copyright © 2022

I0220314

Bernard T. Punzalan, Author

Founder and Principal Investigator

CHamoru Roots Genealogy Project

www.chamorroroots.com

This handbook is dedicated to the indigenous people of the Mariana Islands.

Table of Contents

What is Genealogy?

Genealogy is the study and tracing of a person's, family's', or group of people's ancestral lines[1] and for some, origin. People who engage in genealogy can produce reports and even books to document family history. One common report is a family tree diagram that depicts the relationships between people of several generations within a family. One example of an Ancestral Chart is included in this handbook on page 54.[2]

This is a great opportunity to discover more about your ancestors, embrace your culture, celebrate family traditions, and understand where your ancestors came from. Although genealogy is one of several keys to understanding CHamoru history, we must continue to study Fino' Håya, the ancestral indigenous language of the Taotao Tåno' of Låguas yan Gåni (Mariana Islands), to help us bridge the written or memory record.

Following the trail of Austronesian peoples that have Proto-Malayo-Polynesian linguistic characteristics and current CHamoru DNA studies, the first wave of settlers in Låguas[3], Mariana Islands, occurred sometime between 5,000 and 3,500 years ago from Island Southeast Asia (ISEA), likely from Wallacea (Sulawesi[4] and the Moluccas). They were among the first settlers in Remote Oceania Their mitochondrial DNA (mtDNA) developed uniquely within the haplotypes E2a and E1a2 (Pre-Latte period). Also, there are CHamoru people with mtDNA haplotype B4a1a1a, who are believed to be connected to a separate and second wave of migration to Låguas, which parallels the Latte period.[5]

---

[1] Merriam-Webster dictionary - https://www.merriam-webster.com/dictionary/genealogy
[2] Generated from the CHamoru Roots Genealogy Project website - https://www.chamorroroots.com
[3] Von Chamisso, A. 1821. Remarks and Opinions of the Naturalist of the Expedition, in Otto Von Ktzebue, A Voyage of Discovery into the South Sea and Bering's Straits, translated by H.E. Lloyd, et. al. London, England.
[4] In 2022, research findings from ancient DNA samplings by Rosalind Hunter-Anderson and Joanne Eakin, they reported it is likely that the first wave of settlers came from Sulawesi.
[5] Vilar, M. et al. 2012. The Origins and Genetic Distinctiveness of the Chamorros of the Marianas Islands: An mtDNA Perspective.

Are *Fo'na* (Fu'una) and *Pontan* (Puntan) just legendary myths, or were they the first true settlers of Låguas that somehow got lost in translation and colonization?[6]

---

[6] Fo'na meaning first and Pontan meaning rejuvenated sprout from old, brown coconut. From Brandon Cruz, 2016, "I Tinituhon: Rediscovering Fo'na & Pontan."

Historical Naming Practices and Shifts

It is important to understand the evolution of native naming practices and the influence of colonization in the history of the Mariana Islands. Some of this information may affect or influence the interpretation of data from your research.

Most likely, Taotao Håya, the ancestors of the indigenous people of the Mariana Islands, identified themselves with only a single name before the Spanish Era in the same naming tradition as First Peoples throughout the world. Kinship identify was linked with matrilineal clans. Paternal and maternal surnames in the Mariana Islands did not likely occur until the Spanish began to Christianize the natives.

There are at least three different recordings of naming practices from contact to the early 1800s. One of the earliest recordings was from Fray Juan Pobre. In 1602, Pobre jumped ship and stayed in Luta (Rota) for seven months. During his sojourn he was able to interview Sancho, a Spaniard that was previously marooned in the Mariana Islands and lived among the native inhabitants. Sancho conveyed to Pobre what he had observed and learned of the indigenous people and their culture.[7]

> "When the time comes to get married, as I have said, for the husband and wife to share one house, although they may have been married 20 or 30, if the faithful husband should cheat his live-in wife, and if the latter becomes angry enough, she leaves the house and takes all the children she has with all the furnishings from the house and goes to the house of her parents or relatives and she remains there. In all that time the children do not recognize the father, although he may pass next to them. The husband's relatives must implore her very much before she goes back to him; however, when she cheats on him, it is easier for her to get pardon from the husband because this sin is more serious to males than for females.

---

[7] Pobre, J. (1996). The Story of Fray Juan Pobre's Stay at Rota in the Ladrone Islands in 1602. (R. Levesque trans.), History of Micronesia: First Real Contact, 1596-1637, 3. Quebec, Canada: Levesque Publications

The names which they give themselves from the time they are small are names of fishes or of trees which they use to make their canoes or of other similar things that they value very much."

June 15, 1668, marks the beginning period of Spain colonizing the Mariana Islands. This is precisely when Father Diego San Vitores and other Jesuits backed by a contingent of Spanish Army soldiers planted themselves in the Mariana Islands in the name of Spain. One of the observations of how some of the native males changed their names was recorded by Father Juan Ledesma in 1672.[8]

"When the latter [brothers and nephews of deceased male] inherit [main house and land], they change their names, adopting that of the founder or elder of their family, respecting the distinctions between the high, low and middle lineages to such an extent that it is amazing to see in people with so little diversity in clothing and housing accommodation."

Like what Sancho described to Pobre when a woman divorces her husband, Ledesma clarified that, *"the children follow her and then recognize no other father than the man chosen by their mother as a new husband."* [9]

Both Sancho's and Ledesma's observation supports the notion that although the natives may not have been known to have a surname, their names were dynamic in ancient times. Therefore, some of the natives of the Mariana Islands had more than one name.

As the Jesuits continued recording their experiences, some mentioned the Christian names given to the natives.[10] After being baptized, their Christian name became their

---

[8] Ledsma, J.M.H. (1996). The Native Customs of the Chamorros. (R. Levesque trans), History of Micronesia: Focus on the Mariana Mission, 1670-1673, 5. Quebec, Canada: Levesque Publications
[9] Ibid.
[10] Garcia, F. (2004). The Life and Martyrdom of the Venerable Father Diego Luis de San Vitores, S.J. (M.M. Higgins, F. Plaza and J.M.H. Ledesma, trans). Mangilao, Guam: University of Guam

first name and indigenous name became their surname. Taga became Jose Taga[11], Quipuha became known as Juan Quipuha[12], Aguarin became Diego Aguarin[13], Matå'pang's daughter became known as Maria Assion[14], Soon became Alsono Soon[15], and Hineti became Ignacio Hineti[16].

More than over a century later from Pobre's accounts, it seems that the CHamoru people continued to give their children indigenous names into the early 1800s. This recording occurred in 1819 during the French Uranie expedition visit to the Mariana Islands from Louis Freycinet. The expedition lasted three months in the Mariana Islands. Freycinet recorded that some of the native children were given names based on the talents or personal qualities of their father, or named after fruit, plants, and other things.[17]

At some point during the 1800s, the practice of giving children indigenous names, for the most part, discontinued. For the CHamoru people of Guam, Laura Thompson[18] wrote:

> *"The godfather and godmother or the parents give the child a name. There is no rule for naming the child, but the first boy is usually christened in honor of a deceased grandfather, a first girl in honor of a deceased grandmother. In fact, children are often named after their grandparents or godparents or patron saint*

---

[11] de Viana, A.V. 2005. Pampangos in the Mariana Mission 1668-1684. Micronesian Journal of the Humanities and Social Sciences, 4(1).

[12] Garcia, F. 2004. The Life and Martyrdom of the Venerable Father Diego Luis de San Vitores, S.J. (M.M. Higgins, F. Plaza and J.M.H. Ledesma, trans). Mangilao, Guam: University of Guam

[13] Levesque, R. 1995. History of Micronesia, A Collection of Source Documents, Volume 5 – Focus on the Mariana Mission, 1670-1678. Levesque Publications: Quebec, Canada

[14] Levesque, R. 1997. History of Micronesia, A Collection of Source Documents, Volume 9 – Conquest of the Gani Is, 1687-1696. Levesque Publications: Quebec, Canada

[15] Garcia, F. 2004. The Life and Martyrdom of the Venerable Father Diego Luis de San Vitores, S.J. (M.M. Higgins, F. Plaza and J.M.H. Ledesma, trans). Mangilao, Guam: University of Guam

[16] Goetzfridt, N. 'José de Quiroga y Losada', referenced August 26, 2012, © 2009 Guampedia™, URL: http://guampedia.com/jose-de-quiroga-y-losada/

[17] Freycinet, L.C. (2003). An Account of the Corvette L'Urainie's Sojourn at the Mariana Islands (translated by G. Barrett, trans.). Commonwealth of the Northern Mariana Islands (CNMI): CNMI Division of Historic Preservation: CNMI

[18] Thompson, L. 1947. Guam and Its People (3rd ed). Binghamton, NY: Vail-Ballou

on whose day they were baptized. Frequently, however, a woman in labor prays to a saint for easy delivery. Then she names the child in honor of the saint."

When the U.S. took over Guam, the U.S. Navy discontinued the Spanish convention naming practices (First name, father's surname, mother's surname) and required the American style (first name, middle name, father's surname). So typically, one would find that a mother's surname was used as a person's middle name.

The author has also observed that for some children who were born out of wedlock during those early years under the U.S., two other different styles of naming were being recorded. The most common is a child being named with the mother's surname twice (first name, middle name = mother's surname, and last name = mother's surname). The other practice would be that the child would simply carry the mother's full maiden name (first name, middle name = mother's maternal surname, and last name = mother's paternal surname). In some cases, it also seemed that some illegitimate male children were given female saint names as their middle names: Francisco Rosa, Joaquin Teresa, Jose Maria, Vicente Ana. Perhaps this practice may have been coincidental and more of the traditional Spanish practice of "es el dia de mi Santo."[19]

For the CHamoru people of the Northern Mariana Islands, in 1954, Alexander Spoehr seems to have well captured the CHamoru naming traditions of the Spanish colonial period, through and into the initial influence of Americanization.

> *"Names.—The name given a Chamorro child is selected by the parents. Most given names among the Saipan Chamorros are of Spanish origin, the familiar "Jesus," "Maria," and "Jose" being favorites in the community. The German, Japanese, and now American periods of administration have also left their mark. During German times, "Herman," "Oscar," "Victor," "Wilhelmina," and "Frida"*

---

[19] Leon Guerrero, Mona-Lisa. 2021. FaceBook comment in response to Bernard Punzalan's post.

came into favor, though these names no longer are selected with as much frequency. In the Japanese period, the Spanish names continued to provide most of the given names. Japanese names do not fit well into the European name system established among the Chamorros, and I recorded no Japanese names given at baptism. According to informants, in Japanese times when a Chamorro went to a Japanese school, he was required to assume a Japanese given name. Students who went on for further training, including those few who went to school in Japan, acquired an entire Japanese name, a process that was looked on with favor by the Japanese authorities as leading to a greater assimilation of Japanese culture. It is doubtful that more than a dozen individuals were affected, however, and they have since resumed their Chamorro names.

Today most Chamorro names are still drawn from the corpus of Spanish-diffused given names. A few names of American origin are making their appearance and others are being Anglicized, for example, "Guillermo" to "William." In most cases single names are given, but a few double combinations have appeared in the last few years, two examples being "Victor Segundo" and "Evelyn Ruth." On the whole, however, the Spanish tradition survives as the main source for given names." [20]

---

[20] Sphoer, A. 2000. Saipan: The Ethnology of a War-Devastated Island (2nd ed.). Saipan, Commonwealth of the Northern Mariana Islands, Division of Historic Preservation

Role of Nicknames and Family Clan Names

Like many other cultures, there are certain names in CHamoru communities that are so very common in numbers. It becomes difficult to determine, which Maria or Jose Cruz may be the subjects of discussion. Below are tables of the top 10 common names that were transcribed from each of the population census of Guam from 1920 to 1940.[21]

SURNAMES		
1920	**1930**	**1940**
Cruz	Cruz	Cruz
Santos	Santos	Santos
San Nicolas	San Nicolas	Perez
Perez	Leon Guerrero	San Nicolas
Leon Guerrero	Perez	Castro
Camacho	Castro	Leon Guerrero
Castro	Salas	Sablan
Aguon	Camacho	Duenas
Mendiola	Sablan	Camacho
Salas	Mendiola	Aguon

Table 1

FEMALE NAMES		
1920	**1930**	**1940**
Maria	Maria	Maria
Ana	Ana	Ana
Dolores	Rosa	Rosa
Rosa	Dolores	Dolores
Antonia	Carmen	Carmen
Carmen	Rita	Rita

---

[21] Tables were first published in Punzalan, B. 2022. 1940 Population Census of Guam: Transcribed. Chamorro Roots Genealogy Project.

Josefa	Antonia	Concepcion
Rita	Concepcion	Isabel
Concepcion	Josefa	Antonia
Joaquina	Isabel	Rosario

Table 2

MALE NAMES		
1920	**1930**	**1940**
Jose	Jose	Jose
Juan	Juan	Juan
Vicente	Jesus	Jesus
Jesus	Vicente	Vicente
Joaquin	Francisco	Francisco
Francisco	Joaquin	Joaquin
Antonio	Antonio	Antonio
Manuel	Pedro	Pedro
Pedro	Manuel	Manuel
Ignacio	Ignacio	Ignacio

Table 3

Even the Social Security Administration (SSA) publishes a table for the top first names for births in Puerto Rico and all other territories combined from 1998 to 2021. The other territories: American Samoa, Guam, Northern Mariana Islands, and the U. S. Virgin Islands are less populated and have relatively few births, so the SSA aggregated the popular names. Therefore, there is no way yet to ascertain from SSA's website the top popular names specifically for Guam or the CNMI.

Website: https://www.ssa.gov/oact/babynames/territories.html

While there seems to be very little publications in academia on CHamoru nicknames and family clan names from the Mariana Islands, two of the most notable writings in the public come from Gertrude "Trudis Alemån"[22] Hornbostel cited in Laura Thompson[23], "Archaeology of the Mariana Islands," and Anthony "Malia" Ramirez, "Chamorro Nicknames," republished in Guampedia.com. How CHamoru people are referenced in a CHamoru conversation or even in funeral announcements are very helpful clues to identifying people. It is important to document the nicknames and family clan names in family genealogy.

Thompson, in 1932, noted that most "Guamanians" are not known by their names but by their nicknames. Again, this supports the cultural practice theory that CHamoru people can be known by more than one name.

In Thompson[24]:

> "Concerning nicknames, Mrs. Hornbostel writes: Among the Tsamoros it is the nickname that is used to designate a person, but if he happens to have a real, ancient T'samoro name he goes by the real name and does not have a nickname. For instance, if I ask the first person I meet where I can buy some eggs, he may say, "As Marian Aflleje" ("At Maria of Aflleje's" -Aflleje being a real Tsamoro name) which means that Maria is a daughter of the illustrious family of Aflleje and still retains her family name whether she is married or not. Now suppose that she were married, and I had asked the question of a man from her immediate neighborhood, who did not know that I lived in a different part of town. He might answer, "As Marian Juan" (At Juan's Maria," Juan being the name of Maria's husband). Then I would ask, "Which Marian Juan?" The answer would be either "Marian Aflleje" or "Marian Juan Doddo," meaning that she is the wife of Juan who is a member of the family of Doddo. To designate a married man, he would say, "Juan Maria" or "Juan Marian Aflleje," or if Juan were single, "Juan Doddo." The

---

[22] Alemån means German. Gertrude Constenoble Hornbostel was German. She learned and documented the CHamoru language and culture.
[23] Thompson, Laura. 1932. Archaeology of the Mariana Islands. Bishop Museum Bulletin 100. Honolulu: The Museum.
[24] Ibid.

children might carry on either name, but usually the name of the family which is the richest or the most well-known is used."

Ramirez[25] provides an excellent primer on CHamoru family clan names. They are a way of identifying specific families tied to a larger family tree. According to Ramirez, family nicknames tend to be derived from a reference of at least one of the following ten categories below. For example, the nickname may be a reference to:

- a first name (*CHe'* derived from Jose de la Cruz Anderson)
  Basic rule: traditional CHamoru nicknames are derived from the end of names[26];
- a surname (*Robat* derived from Roberts/Roberto);
- a place name (*Umåtak* derived from Umatac/Garrido);
- an animal (*Kichu*/Fish refers to Lizama);
- a descriptive action or quality (*Ma'fongfong*/To be pounded refers to Manibusan);
- an object (*Åpu*/Ashes refers to Flores);
- a food (*Chåda*/Eggs refers to Cruz);
- a status (*Kabesa*/Leader refers to Flores);
- a body part (*Gugat*/Muscle refers to Santos);
- some other category (*Gualafun*/Full moon refers to Chargualaf)

In Topping, Ogo and Dungca[27], there are many examples of nicknames that were supplied by Rufino Tudela of Saipan and added to their Chamorro-English Dictionary book. The purpose for including the nicknames was to demonstrate that most CHamoru nicknames tend to evolve from using the latter part of a given name. Granted, there are

---

[25] Ramirez, A. 1984. Chamorro Nicknames, retrieved June 9, 2022, from
https://www.guampedia.com/chamorro-nicknames/
[26] Forbes, E. 2011. Chamorro Nicknames, retrieved June 19, 2022, from:
http://paleric.blogspot.com/2011/10/chamorro-nicknames.html
[27] Topping, D. Ogo, P.M. & Dungca, B.C. 1975. Chamorro-English Dictionary. The University Press of Hawaii: Honolulu, Hawaii

exceptions, however, this is worth being mindful of since some CHamoru family clan names are derivatives of first names. This may also further explain how some clan names today, might be actual derivatives of ancient clan names.

Whether the person is referred to with a nickname or a family clan name, each instance has a story of origin and meaning as to how that name came to life. Capturing that story and meaning reveals part of that person's history. The late Joseph Anthony Castro Duenas, a popular CHamoru singer was known as "JD Crutch," because he had to use crutches after contracting polio as a child.[28] James Perez Viernes wrote about the origins of the manggåfan Ducket linked to the late and former Commissioner from Santa Rita, Juan Namauleg Perez:

> *"He married Maria San Nicolas in 1937 and began working as a Room Boy at the U.S. Marine Barracks in Sumay…While working at the Marine Barracks, he got into an argument with an American soldier with the last name Ducket. Perez admits that he was a "very naughty boy" at the time, and as the argument became more heated, Ducket began to chase Perez around the barracks, never catching up to him. From then on, the people of Sumay gave Perez the nickname "Ducket."*[29]

Thompson noted the practices of several fishermen groups, usually comprised of family relatives, who made their living in that manner. The group was known by the nickname of its skilled master, for example "Tembat," "Tugong," or "Dongat." The master would not only pass on his skill to his son, but also his nickname, who in turn becomes the skilled master.[30]

---

[28] Cunningham, J. n.d. Joseph "JD Crutch" Duenas, retrieved June 9, 2022, from https://www.guampedia.com/joseph-j-d-crutch-duenas/
[29] Viernes, J.P. 2008. Fanhasso I Taotao Sumay: Displacement, Dispossession, and Survival in Guam (Thesis). Accessed June 9, 2022, from: http://issuu.com/guampedia/docs/viernes_thesis/1?e=0
[30] Thompson, L. 1947. Guam and Its People. Princeton University Press. Princeton, NJ.

The author of this handbook is a descendant of manggåfan Jai. Orthographically, it would be spelled Yai. In two historical accounts from the 1600s the names Yay and Yai are mentioned. It is currently unknown if there is any connection between the Jai clan and the two young men in the 1600s. However, these names have been flagged as potential ancestors of the Jai clan. Notes of their story have been recorded in the event a connection is later established.

The first account is with Matias Yay who was one of three young CHamorus identified as fervent Christians from among the nobility of the CHamoru people. They were selected by San Vitores to embark on the Buena Socorro for Manila from Guam on June 13, 1671. From Manila they left to New Spain [Mexico]. Pedro Guiran, Yay's brother[31], unfortunately died during the voyage. Ignacio Osi and Matias Yay made it to Mexico and returned back to Guam in 1675.[32] Apparently, Yay along with Osi eventually turned against the Spaniards during Yura's uprising. Yay was captured on October 8, 1684.[33] No other information could be found on Yay thereafter.

The second account of information is very short. It identifies a Yai as one of five CHamorus mentioned by Juan Tilpe in a June 13, 1689, letter to Father Antonio Xaramillo.[34] Tilpe was thanking Xaramillo for showing his mercy and charity to them while on their trip to the Philippines. No other information is found on him and whether he is the same person as Matias Yay aforementioned.

Some other articles and reports that were published and provide additional insight on CHamoru family clan names and nicknames include:

[31] Garcia. 2004. The Life and Martyrdom of the Venerable Father Diego Luis de San Vitores, S.J. (M.M. Higgins, F. Plaza and J.M.H. Ledesma, trans). Mangilao, Guam: University of Guam.
[32] Rogers, R. 1995. Destiny's Landfall: A History of Guam. University of Hawaii: Honolulu, HI
[33] Augusto V. de Viana. 2011. Belgian Missionaries in 17th Century Marianas: The Role of Fr. Peter Coomans and Fr. Gerard Bouwens. Philippiniana Sacra, 46(136):85-109.
[34] Levesque, R. 1997. History of Micronesia, A Collection of Source Documents, Volume 9 – Conquest of the Gani Is, 1687-1696. Levesque Publications: Quebec, Canada

1. Onedera, Peter. 2020. AKAs are steeped in indigenous history. The Guam Daily Post. https://www.postguam.com/forum/featured_columnists/akas-are-steeped-in-indigenous-history/article_66c51a9a-fef2-11ea-8a6c-5735962e1939.html

2. Palomo, A. 1964. The Art of Name-Giving: Those Guamanian Nicknames! Pacific Profile. Guam.

3. Punzalan, Bernard. 2014. I Nå'an Manggåfan Taotao Håya: Chamorro Family Clan Names. Academia.edu https://www.academia.edu/36201434/I_N%C3%85AN_MANGG%C3%85FAN_T AOTAO_H%C3%85YA_CHAMORRO_FAMILY_CLAN_NAMES

4. Punzalan, Bernard. 2014. Chamorro Roots – Håle' CHamoru, First Name-Nickname Dictionary (First Annual Report). Academia.edu https://www.academia.edu/36209845/Chamorro_Roots_Hale_CHamoru_First_N ame_Nickname_Dictionary_First_Annual_Report

5. ___. 2019. A Family with Any Other Name. Minagåhet Blog. http://minagahet.blogspot.com/2019/06/a-family-with-any-other-name.html

There is also an electronic family clan name report that is accessible and can be generated from the CHamoru Roots Genealogy Project website.[35]

Can you identify how names or nicknames you or other family members are known by?

---

[35] Accessible only to subscribers with a minimum of database permission. https://www.chamorroroots.com/tng13/showreport.php?reportID=7

Role of Traditional Place Names

Again, because the two most popular names within the 1920, 1930 and 1940 census of Guam were Maria Cruz and Jose Cruz[36], like nicknames and family clan names, traditional place names can make a big difference with helping to pinpoint which Cruz is the subject of the conversation or research. In some cases, we might find that certain place names, may also be tied to family clan names.

Therefore, depending on the conversation and the relationship between the sender and receiver, Maria Cruz may now be referred to as Maria Ma'fongfong, Marian Ignacion Yai or Marian Yai gi Palai. Again, there may be other possibilities, but this example illustrates the utility of place names and how CHamoru people sometimes reference others in their communications.

Throughout the history of the Mariana Islands, the ancestral traditional place names and locations have been consistently static whenever mentioned in publications or referenced in discussions. However, some place names have evolved to encompass a politically larger, or in some cases, a smaller geographic area, which may be sometimes designated as a village, barrio, city, town, municipality, or district that may encompass several other place names tied to a political jurisdiction or population. Unfortunately, many traditional place names are forgotten.

The Hornbostels, who studied the Mariana Islands in the 1920s, indicated that there are thousands of place names in the Mariana Islands.[37] They theorized, "One method of approach to the problem of the origin and migrations of the peoples of the Pacific lies in the study of place names." In 2011, Anthony Sanchez put it aptly that place names are descriptive. They describe areas in a manner that is commonly understood.[38] Although,

---

[36] Punzalan, B. 2022. 1940 Population Census of Guam: Transcribed. Chamorro Roots Genealogy Project.
[37] Hornbostel, G. and H. 1926. Chamorro Locality Names in Guam Recorder, February edition.
[38] Sanchez, A. 2011. Guam Place Names Are Descriptive. Pacific Daily News. Retrieved June 16, 2022, from: https://www.newspapers.com/image/214941646

we still do not know the meaning of many ancient native words and place names, progress is being made to study and address these concerns.

In 1944, the Department of Interior's Board on Geographical Names, published a comprehensive list of "Geographical Names in the Mariana Islands."[39] The document listed the name, designation, island, and some had coordinates. Some ancient place names that are mentioned in Levesque's History of Micronesia series do not appear on their list, nevertheless it remains one of the most comprehensive lists available.

Also, Peter Onedera's research, "Nå'an Lugåt Siha Gi Ya Guåhan (Guam Place Names)," was funded in part by a Guam Humanities Council grant. It was published in a booklet by the Kumision i Fino' Chamorro and the Kumision i Nå'an Lugåt in 1989. The booklet was written in CHamoru with English translations identifying names, history and meanings of the village names in Guam. He further translates and conforms the spelling of over 800 places names using the current CHamoru orthography. The current Kumisión I Fino' CHamoru yan Fina'någuen i Historia yan Lina'la' i Taotao Tåno' in Guam has been designated the official Kumisión i Na'an Lugåt. As such, they have embarked on an extensive effort to restore traditional place names and formalize their orthographically aligned spelling and usage. The Kumisión is recognized as the leading authority on traditional place names in Guam.

It is interesting to review land records from 1890-1906 that were digitized and now available on www.familysearch.org. These records are another resource to help bridge some genealogy knowledge gaps between the 1897 Census (last Spanish Government

---

[39] ____. 1944. Decisions Rendered - United States, Department of the Interior, Board on Geographical Names, Issues 4401-4412, Geographical Names in the Mariana Islands pg 60-86. Accessed June 16, 2022, from: https://books.googleusercontent.com/books/content?req=AKW5Qae5Zn7Ae-KTUpeppZrtnFhsgxm0FDU8IIYxvhdL4IIUBRH6P5Iu7YCO5_I3zJFkmj3YsFzGieFpDvKWYojFQx73QA75ZKplUHuvsy99YmlgzduYq7Z2ynL6TfyUhP7vL-8pCq4wOl9j07BvV5m1S9awaoLilbPc7BbM3bUuiEZLsH_3_ZHKIxllaB3KkiIQn0S0YAb5J6-DlgGXxpSC-ApN2Bcb81A5wF-ePHaluvIBsKZFsuinK-QMUv7KtfUMnTXvQBXHHGNS9CWzYUq9G6IPqKExm1LmWnES07Jn4_QBRnBqdJo}

Census) and Guam Newsletters (contained vital statistics beginning in 1914) to the 1920 Census.

Each land estate record is described to a certain extent, which often includes identifying the place name and bordering properties to the north, south, east and west. As such, if the bordering properties were owned or being cultivated by a known person, that person would also be named. And, in some cases, these land records included the person's family clan name.

Digging deep within the manuscripts or letters written by the Jesuits in the 1600s, they record some of the place names where some events occurred, and in some cases the name of the CHamoru person involved. For example:

Maga'låhi Andres Resu/Ressu was the Fiscal of *Finna, Guam* around 1690. His wife, also a native, was **Doña Sabina Tenni**.[40] The Catholic mission proudly boasted that this married couple (they suffered from a bad heart and without remedy) through the advice of Father Gerardo Bouvens/Bouwens, Parish Priest of Finna, promised to attend confession and communion on every feast-day of Our Lady. Because they were loyal and performed with exactitude, they purportedly became free of their illness.[41]

Fena (Fenna)[42] is no longer a village, but its place name remains along with some of the archeological remnants of the past; at least the ones that were not destroyed or displaced

---

[40] Spelling of names and places are retained as extracted from the source.

[41] Levesque, R. 1997. History of Micronesia, A Collection of Source Documents, Volume 9 – Conquest of the Gani Is, 1687-1696. Levesque Publications: Quebec, Canada

[42] Freycinet, C. 2003. An Account of the Corvette L'Urainie's Sojourn at the Mariana Islands (translated by Glynn Barrett). CNMI Division of Historic Preservation: CNMI. Freycinet also recorded a list of past and present ancient place names, but not as extensive as the Department of Interior's.

from the man-made Fena Lake reservoir. For families that may have owned property in this area, examples like this may serve as genealogy clues.

Can you name the traditional place names of where you or your family and ancestors may have resided or currently reside?

Impact from Colonization

As previously mentioned, when CHamoru people were converted to Christianity through baptism, CHamorus assumed a Christian first name. The CHamoru name originally held became a surname. This is evidenced in the 1727 Census of the Marianas, which is the very first census of the Mariana Islands recorded with names. It is common to find a father, mother, brother, or sister all having different surnames. Unless one's family unit was recorded by either the Spanish or other European record, or perhaps survived oral history within a family, it is difficult to trace family lineages prior to the 1800s.

Families tied to either the *mañakilo* (high class) clans or with strong Spanish bloodlines deeply rooted in history such as the Torres family, likely have a better chance of tracing their genealogy prior to the 1800s. While the Catholic Church may also have vital records for recording sacraments such as baptisms and marriages, many records may have been destroyed during World War II or during typhoons.

There were long periods of gaps in census efforts like from the 1727 census to 1758 census there is a gap of 31 years; from the 1758 census to 1897 census there is 139-year gap; and then from 1897 census to 1920 census not only a 23-year gap but also a transition of colonial powers from Spain to the United States. These gaps, make it even more difficult for families whose ancestors may have emigrated elsewhere from the 1800s to the early 1900s.

Another challenge in researching CHamoru genealogy is that there is a Spanish tradition and influence on how names were recorded. In traditional Spanish practice the person's name would be a first name immediately followed by the father's surname and lastly followed by the mother's surname. For example, the name "Matias Espinosa Leon Guerrero," as it is known today, is understood as Matias' father's surname "Leon Guerrero" and his mother's surname "Espinosa." But during the Spanish era his name is recorded as "Matias de Leon Guerrero y Espinosa."

On March 4, 1920, Naval Captain William W. Gilmer, a governor of Guam, decreed that all residents of Guam sixteen years and older must register and obtain a cèdula personal, which was basically a certificate of Identification. The purpose for creating these documented identification cards was to enable a person to perform transactions with the government such as tax payments, land transfers, birth registrations, court matters, and so on. Another purpose was to reduce the centuries-old Spanish custom of a child possessing the father's last name first and the mother's maiden name second and reduce the practice of double names, (i.e. changing the name of what may once been "Matias de Leon Guerrero y Espinosa" to "Matias Espinosa Leon Guerrero"). This brings naming practices in line with the Western tradition of the father's name being recorded as the official surname.

For one reason or another not everyone's name was converted. The result of this naming protocol change left some people officially carrying their mother's maiden name as their surname. There are some brothers and sisters even today, where one has the mother's last name, and another has the father's last name stemming from the inconsistent application of this naval decree. For instance, Matias Espinosa Leon Guerrero's sister Juanita, hypothetically, may have ended up with the name Juanita Leon Guerrero Espinosa. In some cases, on Guam, the "Leon" was dropped from "Leon Guerrero," and some families now carry only the "Guerrero" surname, making it even more difficult to research.

A few causes for the spelling variations of names in recorded documents include convenience and influence. Some middle names were used in place of surnames because they were easier to say or pronounce in English. Likewise, the author observed that some names seemed phonetically spelled out during the early U.S. census periods.

In the February 1926 edition of the Guam Recorder, the publishers were not shy about writing the following article because it was convenient for them:

"AMERICAN NAMES FOR CHAMORRO CHILDREN

The matter of identification among the native inhabitants of Guam becomes more and more problematic every day. The cause of which is the similarity of names; both in Christian, middle and surname.

To facilitate the proper keeping of civil records, and to make identification among the native inhabitants of Guam less entangling, it is thought wise to make this suggestion to the fathers and mothers of Guam *to give American names to their newly born children.*

This is a measure taken to prevent any possible confusion in the identification of natives of Guam in the future in case of legal requirements. To this end, it is believed that much of this remedial step can be accomplished through the kind support of everyone, especially the clergy to whom the child is brought for baptism."

Today, most indigenous native names are very rare to find in CHamoru families. In addition, the majority of the CHamoru population resides in the U.S.[43] Figure 2 provides a breakdown of the CHamoru population in 2010 in Guam, the CNMI and the U.S. respectively.

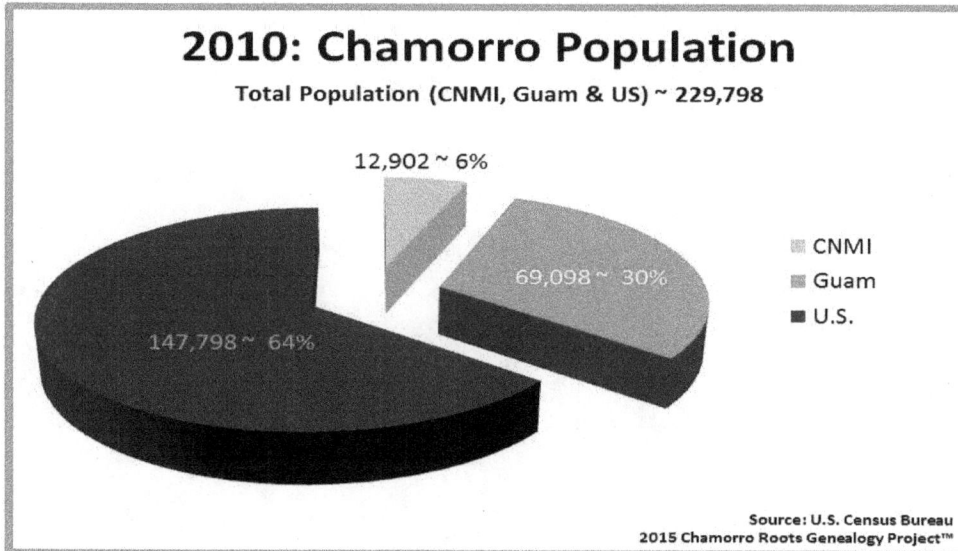

2010: Chamorro Population
Total Population (CNMI, Guam & US) ~ 229,798

12,902 ~ 6%

69,098 ~ 30%

147,798 ~ 64%

- CNMI
- Guam
- U.S.

Source: U.S. Census Bureau
2015 Chamorro Roots Genealogy Project™

Figure 1

---

[43] Punzalan, B. 2019. Technological Milestones in CHamoru Genealogy. MPI. From: https://www.mdpi.com/2313-5778/3/3/38

However, there are families of today that have given their children native first names. The more this is practiced, whether locally or abroad, the better the chances for resurgence.

Dr. Brenna Lorenz, a former professor at the University of Guam, authored, "The Pacific Islander's Book of Name's," which was published in 1996. She included some of the ancient CHamoru names from the 1727 and 1758 census. Professor Rosa Salas Palomo assisted her with the interpretation of some of those names. There is currently an attempt on FaceBook by Lina'la King Camacho[44] and others, unaware of Lorenz's Book, to independently list and define the ancient names recorded in the 1727 and 1758 census.

How might have colonization affected the names in your family tree?

---

[44] Lina'la King Camacho is originally from Tinian, but currently resides in Hawaii. She is the founder and administrator of the FaceBook group "Taotao Mona – Chamorro Ancestry."

How and Where to Begin

When you begin your genealogy journey, always – always, keep in mind that every name has a story. Start with yourself and write what you know about yourself, parents, and siblings.[45] An Individual Genealogy Worksheet, page 45, is provided in this handbook to help you get started. Thereafter, move forward and work toward what you do not know. Find out all the vital information you can about your parents and write it down. Then find out about your grandparents, great-grandparents, and so forth. This handbook also includes a Family Group Worksheet, page 46, and Ancestral Worksheet, page 47, to help you document more about your family and lineage.

Here are some ideas that can help you document a story about yourself. You can even use this to describe your family members.

- Describe some of your physical traits:
    - Color of eyes
    - Color of hair
    - Weight
    - Height
- Religion (past and present)
- Places you have lived
- Places (countries, states, etc.) you have visited and what you experienced
- Schools you attended
- Places you have worked
- Volunteer work
- Other Events in your life
- Health
- Military service
- Favorite things/hobbies
    - Sports

---

[45] Some sections have been reproduced and adapted from the National Archives Records Administration, retrieved June 8, 2022, from https://www.archives.gov/riverside/how-to-begin-genealogical-research

- o Activities
- Awards and recognition
- Skills and abilities
- People you have met
- Things you celebrate
- List some things you know about your culture, or family traditions.

As you can imagine, there may be a lot of information to collect depending on the scope of your genealogy objectives. It could be overwhelming at times. If so, consider limiting the amount information you collect on other family members at the beginning of your journey. Pace yourself so that you are not discouraged by being too overwhelmed.

If necessary, take breaks when conducting your research. Particularly, when things seem to come to a dead end. Many pieces are really parts of a larger puzzle that do not immediately fit but will later.

Keep in mind that in CHamoru genealogy, there are at least five key items from the numerous and varied written resources and oral history accounts: 1) names, 2) family clan names, 3) dates, 4) places, and 5) relationships. These are some of the essential elements of family research. People can be identified in records or conversations by their names, nicknames, family clan names, dates of events in their lives (birth, marriage, death), the places they lived, and by relationships to others, either stated or implied, in the records.

Take inventory, review, and examine the resources that you already possess. Look for information in photos, newspaper clippings, military certificates, birth and death certificates, marriage licenses, naturalization certificates, diaries, letters, scrapbooks, baby books, and many other documents.

If you know some of your relatives, they too are a vital source. Visit, telephone, video conference those in your family who may have information, particularly older relatives.

Perhaps someone else may have already gathered some of the data about the families in which you are interested. Write a letter, make a personal visit, or perform a telephone survey to find out about such persons and what information has already been collected. In addition to possessing vital information, family members may also know family stories that can be collected and preserved for future generations. These might also assist or point you in a certain direction within a certain phase of your research. If you do visit your relatives, try and audio or video record your conversations with them. This will come in very handy for many years to come and other family members will appreciate it.

Reunions are a great way to interview people, share and collect information. Many families are already doing this and have published family trees like the Kabesa, Kotla, Kueto, and Sablan/Zablan families, to name a few. These family tree books are also a great fundraising mechanism to conduct subsequent reunions or offset research costs.

Please record your sources and give credit where credit is due. Recording the source of your information not only acknowledges the source, but also serves as a point of reference for the information, you include in reports. Additionally, it provides a positive credential for your research effort. It will come in handy if you come across conflicting information from another document or source. Unfortunately, it is common to find faulty information repeated over time and throughout multiple documents or other sources. In some cases, because of CHamoru cultural practices, some information from interviews will not jibe with official documents. For example, some families may have raised children from another family, *"mapoksai,"*[46] a historical cultural practice. There may be other reasons why things occurred the way they did. This is typically the difference between oral and written history.

At minimum, consider the following information to include when recording your source of information:

---

[46] See Poksai: Informal Adoption, accessed June 10, 2022, from: https://www.guampedia.com/poksai/

- The name of the person/author/institution of the source
- Date of the source
- Title of the source
- Name of publisher
- Location
- If the source is from a website, record the URL and the date last accessed. The date last accessed is important since the internet is dynamic. Therefore, the link may have changed or may no longer exist.

If you have not done so, consider investing in genealogy software as a tool to record your data in electronic format. Today's technological advances in genealogy software help to document and, in most cases, help you to write your family tree with the capability of producing a variety of customized reports that are even editable after it is generated from the software. While there are a variety of genealogy software available on the market, the two most popular seem to be Reunion for Apple computers and Family Tree Maker for Microsoft Windows users. See the Sample Genealogy Book Report beginning on page 55 that was generated with the Reunion software by the author. Some on-line genealogy sites offer programs to use their services as well.

If you ever consider sharing your electronic data with others, make sure it has the capability to export the data in GEDCOM format, which is the genealogy data standard.[47] Depending on the genealogy software, there are several video tutorials that can be found on YouTube and other sources on the internet that may help guide you through the process with creating and exporting a GEDCOM file as well as importing a GEDCOM file from another source.

---

[47] See GEDCOM, accessed June 10, 2022, from: https://www.gedcom.org/

Places and Sources

<u>Federal Records</u>

The National Archives and Records Administration (NARA) maintains records that are of great use to genealogical researchers. The U.S. federal census, which is taken every ten years since 1790 is a very important source. Thanks to partnerships between NARA and other organizations, all censuses taken more than 72 years ago have been made available to the public on-line. The National Archives and Records Administration also holds records documenting military service, passenger arrival, naturalization, taxation, court actions, land ownership, and much more.

Website: www.archives.gov/research/genealogy/start-research/

For Guam, the first U.S. federal census was conducted in 1920. For the CNMI, the first U.S. federal census was not conducted until 1970. It is also important to note that there were CHamoru people and families that migrated to the U.S. Some were whalers, some were farmers, and some were military, while others sought job opportunities, medical care or change in their living environment.

The Library of Congress also houses some historical records of the Mariana Islands, "Spanish colonial government, Mariana Islands records." Among other documents, one can find hard copies of the 1897 census, vital statistics published in the Guam Newsletters and Guam Recorder. Below is a summary of records:

"Royal decrees, court records, orders to and from the governor, circulars, reports, and other records pertaining to Spanish colonial government in the Mariana Islands. Subjects include agriculture; the Anglo-Spanish War, 1762-1763; building and repair of bridges, military installations, roads, and schools; cattle; church and missionary matters; coffee-growing; colonization; commerce; criminal investigations and proceedings; daily life; education; exploration; fisheries; foreign visitors; grass-roots democracy; economy; hunting; local government for all of the islands, especially Guam; manufacturing; mining; ports; prisons and prisoners; public finance; public health; public welfare; ships, capture of ships, and shipwrecks; urban improvement;

vagrancy; vital statistics; and the water supply system of Manila, Philippines. Individuals and organizations represented include José Casillas Salazar; Felipe María de la Corte y Ruano Calderón; Angel de Pazos y Vela-Hidalgo; the College of San Juan de Letran, Hagåtña, Guam; and the U.S. Consulate, Hagåtña, Guam."
Website: https://lccn.loc.gov/mm78055319

Congressional records also contain information and names of some CHamoru people. The World War II claims efforts lists hundreds of people. Both Guam and CNMI Congressional Delegates have submitted congressional records recognizing CHamoru people by name for their achievements.
Website: https://www.congress.gov/congressional-record

State/Territory Records

Every state/territory also has their own form of archives. State/Territory archives hold records of great value to genealogists. Some of these records include state/territory censuses, military records, land records, court records, prison records, and much more.

1. Department of Land Management (Guam)
   590 S. Marine Corps Drive ITC Building, Ste 733
   Tamuning, Guam 96913
   Phone: (671) 649-5263
   Email: dlmdir@land.guam.gov
   Website: https://dlm.guam.gov
2. Superior Court of Guam
   Guam Judicial Center
   120 West O'Brien Drive
   Hagåtña, Guam 96910-5174
   Records Branch at (671) 475-3449
   Email: scog.records@guamcourts.org
   Website: http://www.guamcourts.org
3. Commonwealth Recorder's Office

Email: Rebecca.Santos@NMIJudiciary.com

Website: https://nmijudiciary.com/index.php/superior/recorders-office-2/

County Records

There are no County Records in Guam and the CNMI; however, there are many records held by the individual counties in each state. Some of these include deed records, probate records, criminal and civil court records, tax records, and voting records. All these records have the potential for being good sources of genealogical data. Such records are normally in the county courthouses although some original documents have been filmed by different organizations and can be viewed elsewhere. The earliest county records or copies of them, often, are available in state archives.

Birth, Marriage, and Death Records

Both Commonwealth of the Mariana Islands (CNMI) and Guam have forms available on-line to request for copies of certain vital records.

1. CNMI certified birth and death records:

   https://www.chcc.health/healthvitalstatistics.php

2. Guam. Application for copy of birth, death or marriage certificate on Guam:

   http://www.govguamdocs.com/dphss/docs/VitalStatistics/ApplicationforCopyofBirthMarriageDeathCertificate.pdf

   Office of Vital Statistics (Guam)

   Rancare Commercial Buildispan

   761 S. Marine Corp Drive

   Tamuning, GU 96913

   Phone: (671) 300-9263

   Email: maria.quinata@dphss.guam.gov

   Website: https://dphss.guamdev.com/dph/office-of-vital-statistics/

Within the United States, some states began to keep records of births and deaths earlier, but for most of the United States, birth and death registration became a requirement between 1890 and 1915. Before that time, these events, generally will be found recorded only in church records and some in family bibles. Most marriages can be found recorded in county records, which sometimes date to the establishment of the county.

Church Records

Investigate the possibility of finding genealogical data in the records of the church to which your ancestor or family belonged. A few churches have records of important events in the lives of members, such as sacrament records, and provide valuable information for family historians. Keep in mind that many historical records may have been destroyed from World War II or natural disasters. Also, Churches are not under any obligation to provide genealogical information.

Cemeteries

Do not overlook funeral home records, cemetery records, and gravestone inscriptions. Likewise, articles, obituaries and funeral announcements published in the media are a great source. In Guam, there are some family private cemeteries. Please respect the wishes of each family if they chose not to disclose or confirm any information.

Cemetery	Location
Bordallo Family Cemetery	Private
Calvo Compound Cemetery	Private
Custino Family Cemetery	Agana, Guam
Guam Memorial Park	Barrigada, Guam
Guam Veterans Cemetery	Piti, Guam
Guam Windward Memorial	Windward Hills, Guam
Holy Cross Catholic (Togcha) Cemetery	Togcha, Guam
Merizo Catholic Cemetery	Merizo, Guam
Mount Carmel Catholic Cemetery	Agat, Guam
Old Agat Cemetery	Agat, Guam
Our Lady of Peace Memorial	Windward Hills, Guam

Pedro Pangelinan Martinez Family Cemetery	Private
Perez Family Cemetery	Private
Pigo Catholic Cemetery	Anigua, Guam
Rest Haven Cemetery	Talofofo, Guam
Saint Joseph Catholic Cemetery	Inarajan, Guam
Sumay Cemetery	Naval Station, Guam
U.S. Naval Cemetery	Agana, Guam
Umatac Cemetery	Umatac, Guam
Vicente A. Limtiaco Memorial (Tiguag) Cemetery	Nimitz Hill, Guam

Table 4

Cemetery	Location
CNMI Veterans Cemetery	Marpi, Saipan
Mount Carmel Cemetery	Chalan Kanoa, Saipan
San Jose Cemetery	San Jose, Tinian
Sanctuario Memorial Gardens	Kagman, Saipan
Simenteyon San Jose	Songsong, Rota
Tanapag Cemetery	Tanapag, Saipan

Table 5

Libraries, Societies, and Archives

Libraries, family history centers, historical and genealogical societies and non-government archival repositories are all good sources for genealogical and family history data and may hold things such as newspapers, private papers of individuals, and records of private organizations. Some of these organizations may have workstations that can be used to access on-line genealogy websites or resources without charge and would otherwise require paid subscriptions to access.

Resources on Guam

1. Guam Family History Center

    1088 Marine Corps Drive, Dededo, Phone: 671-487-7098,

E-mail: tamiburton671@gmail.com

Website: https://www.familysearch.org/en/wiki/Guam_Online_Genealogy_Records

Links:

- 1897 Census:
  https://www.familysearch.org/search/image/index?owc=M62H-Y68%3A13862301%3Fcc%3D1392581
- Judicial Records:
  https://www.familysearch.org/search/image/index?owc=M62H-Y68%3A13862301%3Fcc%3D1392581
- Land Records:
  https://www.familysearch.org/search/image/index?owc=M62H-T68%3A13861701%3Fcc%3D1392581
- Obituaries:
  https://www.familysearch.org/search/image/index?owc=M62H-T29%3A13861801%3Fcc%3D1392581

2. Nieves Flores Memorial Library (Guam Public Library)

   65 Follard Street

   Agana, Guam

   Phone: 671-475-4753

   Email: gpls@gpls.guam.gov

   Website: https://gpls.guam.gov/

3. Richard F. Taitano Micronesia Area Research Center, Mangilao, Guam

   UOG Station

   Mangilao, Guam 96923

   Office: 671-735-2150/2151

   Website: https://www.uog.edu/marc-home

   - Genealogy Collection: Dr. Monique Storie mstorie@triton.uog.edu
     or Dr. Melissa Taitano, marcref@triton.uog.edu
     There are also hard copies of the Guam Newsletter (1909-1922) and
     Guam Recorder (1924-1940) that contains vital statistic information listing
     marriages, births and deaths.

- Spanish Documents & Manuscript Collections (includes Index cards by Dr. Jane Underwood: Professor Omaira Brunal-Perry, obrunal@triton.uog.edu

- Index to the Judicial Records of Guam, Spanish Language Records 1807-1920 and English Language Records 1907-1935, By Omaira Brunal-Perry, Marjorie G. Driver, M. S. Taitano, William L. Wuerch (Media format: CD, System requirements: PC; Windows 3.1/95; CD-ROM drive.)

Some On-line Resources

The internet is the world at your fingertips. Leverage it as a tool to identify other potential resources. Again, please understand that the internet and websites are very dynamic. Some of the links may be out of date and no longer accessible. If that is the case, use an internet search engine (i.e., Google, Bing, etc.) to see if the information still exists but with a newer link. Again, once you start your research, record your sources. Your personal list of sources will grow like your family tree.

Also, social media sources such as FaceBook are a great source for connecting with family and distant family members. Many already maintain family group pages.

Blog:

    Påle' Eric: http://paleric.blogspot.com/

    Påle' Eric Forbes, OFM Capuchin, is a CHamoru historian and genealogist and maintains an excellent blog filled with several categorical topics on the CHamoru people and Mariana Islands history.

Cemeteries:

1. Billion Graves: www.billiongraves.com

   Billion Graves is a large resource for searchable GPS cemetery data.

2. Find a Grave: www.findagrave.com

   Find a Grave is a website that allows the public to search and add to an online database of cemetery records.

Genealogy:

1. Ancestry: www.ancestry.com

   Ancestry is a genealogy website that currently manages about 10,000 terabytes of data, including records detailing births, marriages, deaths, military service, immigration, census, member family trees, DNA testing and much more. You will find many family trees with CHamoru people. Some are public and some you must contact the person that maintains the family tree for access.

2. CHamoru Roots Genealogy Project: www.chamorroroots.com

   Pertinent data and publications:

   - Database over 390,000 names
   - Census transcriptions/indices
     - 1727 Census Index
     - 1758 Census Index
     - 1920 Census Transcription and Index
     - 1930 Census Transcription and Index
     - 1940 Census Transcription and Index
   - Alphabetical Index of Names Contained in Dr. Jane H. Underwood's Guam Genealogy Database
   - List of Orphans in Sumay, Guam. (Circa 1890s)
   - #Weavers & #Net Makers from the 1920 to 1940 Census: Alphabetical Index
   - Index of Names – Guam Land Records (1895-1906)
   - Chamorro Roots – Hale' CHamoru, First Name-Nickname Dictionary (First Annual Report)
   - I Na'an Manggafan Taotao Haya: Chamorro Family Clan Names

3. Fold3: www.fold3.com

   Fold3® features premier collections of original military records. These records include the stories, photos, and personal documents of the men and women who served in the military. Many of the records come from the U.S. National archives, The National Archives of the U.K. and other international records.

4. Geni: www.geni.com

   Geni is also a genealogy website where you can find member family trees that some CHamoru people use.

5. Heritage Quest Online: www.heritagequestonline.com

   Heritage Quest offers a comprehensive genealogical resource.

6. USGenweb Project: www.usgenweb.org

   USGenWeb provides and contains free websites for researchers to share their genealogical research.

History & Humanities:

1. CNMI Humanities Council has a digital archive with excellent sources available on their website: https://www.nmhcouncil.org/

   - Digital archive: https://www.nmhcouncil.org/digital-archive/
   - Records of the Spanish Government in the Mariana Islands: https://www.nmhcouncil.org/wp-content/uploads/archives/spanish
   - CNMI Archives' Oral History Project: https://archives.marianas.edu/medialist.php
   - How to Conduct Oral History Interviews[48] (Rlene Santos Steffy. 2020): https://www.nmhcouncil.org/wp-content/uploads/HowToConductOralHistoryInterviews.pdf

2. Dipattamenton I Kaohao Guinahan Chamorro (Department of CHamoru Affairs): https://dca.guam.gov/

3. Guam Council on Arts and Humanities: https://www.guamcaha.org/

4. Guampedia is Guam's on-line encyclopedia: https://www.guampedia.com

5. Kumision i Fino' CHamoru yan i Fina'nå'guen i Historia yan i Lina'la' i Taotao Tåno' (The Commission on CHamoru Language and the Teaching of the History and Culture of the Indigenous People of Guam): https://kumisionchamoru.guam.gov/

Direct link access to some of the Census documents for Guam.

---

[48] In 2020, Rlene Santos Steffy and the CNMI Humanities Council produced and published, How to Conduct Oral History Interviews. The book is much more detailed than this handbook and a very informative guide.

- FamilySearch.org 1897 Census:
  https://www.familysearch.org/search/image/index?owc=M62H-Y68%3A13862301%3Fcc%3D1392581
- Internet Archive: Guam Census 1920:
  https://archive.org/details/14thcensusofpopu2032unit
- Internet Archive: Guam Census 1920 SoundEx Cards:
  https://archive.org/details/soundex1920gu001
- Internet Archive: Guam Census 1930:
  https://archive.org/details/15thcensus2629unit/page/n2/mode/1up
- National Archives: Guam Census 1940:
  https://1940census.archives.gov/search/?search.page=1&search.result_type=image&search.state=GU#searchby=location&searchmode=browse&year=1940
- National Archives: Guam Census 1950:
  https://1950census.archives.gov/search/?page=1&state=GU

Newspapers:
1. Guam Pacific Daily News: www.guampdn.com
2. Marianas Variety: www.mvariety.com
3. Newspapers: www.newspapers.com

   Newspapers is an online archive of newspapers. It includes electronic copies of the Guam Daily News and Guam Pacific Daily News.
4. Saipan Tribune: https://www.saipantribune.com/
5. The Guam Daily Post: https://www.postguam.com/

Obituaries:

Legacy: www.legacy.com

   Legacy is a global network of online obituaries.

Other:

Cyndi's List: www.cyndislist.com

Cyndi's List contains a plethora of genealogy sites on the Internet. It is a categorized and cross-referenced list of links for genealogical research. The site contains roughly 332,000 links in more than 200 categories.

What other websites would you add to this list?

Oral Family History Interviews

Recording oral histories is a very effective way of capturing information that is difficult to obtain by any other means.[49] One can leverage oral accounts to complement other kinds of information. While a picture may be worth a thousand words, a person being interviewed will be able to tell the story behind what may have been captured in a photo and provide the names of the people. Recorded interviews also have the benefit of capturing the interviewees' voices and, if video recordings are made, those persons' moving images, too. Indeed, it is exciting to listen to the actual voices and viewing the moving images of our family elders.

<u>Preparing and Conducting the Interview</u>
1. Determine what your goal is for the interview.
2. Prepare and learn as much as you can about the person you are going to interview.
   a. Has any other family member or anyone else already conducted research or interview?
   b. Determine whether there are members of the family who have the information you are interested in discovering, and, if they are willing and able to share it with you during a recorded interview.
   c. Are there other documents or photos pertinent to your interview that you can share with the interviewee?
3. What resources will be used to record the interview?
4. What will happen to the recordings and other documentary materials after the interview?
   a. Should the materials be preserved and made available to other members of the family and others? If so, would it be desirable to preserve the materials in a public repository, such as a library, archive, or museum? It is important to discuss this with prospective repositories at the start of the project because

---

[49] Reproduced and adapted from the Library of Congress, The American Folk Life Center, Oral History Interviews: accessed June 8, 2022, from: https://loc.gov/folklife/familyfolklife/oralhistory.html

they may have specific requirements, such as the use of certain media for interviews and the use of certain release forms that will be signed by interviewers and interviewees.

b. It is strongly recommended that a repository be identified prior to beginning the project as the long-term cost of preserving oral history recordings are very high.

a. Consider using a release form. In today's world of legalities, it is a good idea to have one. If not, and you are able to record the interview, use the text of the release form to obtain the interviewee's acknowledgement and permission. A sample release form originally from the Library of Congress' American Folklife Center's publication Folklife and Fieldwork: A Layman's Introduction to Field Techniques is included in this handbook.

5. Be respectful and cognizant of the interviewee's time and condition. Plan to keep your interviews to a reasonable length. A typical length for an interview is between one and one and a half hours. It is the interviewer's responsibility to determine if the interview should be concluded because the interviewee may be fatigued or for any other reason.

6. Other tips before, during and after the interview:

   a. When you reach out to the interviewee, clearly and accurately explain to who you are, why you want to do the interview, and what will happen to the information you collect from that person.

   b. Be yourself. Don't pretend to know more about something than you do know.

   c. Never record secretly.

d. Before you start recording, try to find a location that's conducive to producing a clear recording. For example, if the recording session is taking place at the interviewee's home, choose a room that is farther away from the street to cut down on noise created by traffic.

e. At the start of the recording, make a brief opening announcement that specifies date and place of the interview, names of the interviewer and interviewee, and the general topic of the interview. For example:

Today is Wednesday, June 8, 2022. This is the start of an interview with Rosa Leon Guerrero Cruz, at her home in the village of Tamuning, next to the location of the old Drive-in. My name is Bernard Punzalan and I'll be the interviewer. I am Tan Rosa's grandson, and this interview is being done in connection with the history of the manggåfan Jai and Mafongfong family. We will mainly be talking about my grandmother's recollection of the family when they lived in Pålai, Piti before the war.

This is very useful information that can be used to identify the basic circumstances of the interview later.

f. Keep the audio recorder or video camera running throughout the interview. Don't turn the machine on and off except when asked to do so or when an interruption requires it.

g. During the interview, encourage your interviewee by paying attention. Keep any time spent looking at a list of questions or adjusting the recording equipment to a minimum.

h. Keep questions short. Avoid complicated multi-part questions.

i. Never ask a question you don't understand.

j. Avoid asking questions "yes" or "no," questions.

k. Avoid asking leading questions that suggest answers. For example, instead of asking "Was Pålai, Piti a great place to live before the war?" Rather, ask: "How would you describe life in Pålai, Piti before the war?"

l. Keep your opinions out of the interview.

m. Try not to begin the interview with questions about controversial subjects.

n. Don't interrupt your interviewee's answers. Use non-verbal communication (eye-contact and nodding) to encourage the interviewee.

o. Use follow-up questions to elicit more detailed information. For example: When did that happen? Did that happen to you? What did you think about that? What are the steps in doing that? Can you give me an example of that? What happened next?

p. Be prepared to let your interviewee take the discussion off in different directions. This can sometimes lead to unexpected and exciting discoveries.

q. Make the recording as complete and accurate a record of the interview as you can. If you are using only an audio recorder, remember that it has no visual aspect. Therefore, if the interviewee makes a significant gesture — holds her/his hands apart and says, "It was about this long," for example — be sure to follow up with a question that allows the information to be captured on the recording verbally: "So, was it about two feet long?"

r. Put a brief closing announcement on the tape at the end of the interview. For example:

This is the end of the June 8, 2022, interview with Rosa Leon Guerrero Cruz. The interviewer was Bernard Punzalan.

s. Save the interview recording so it can be accessed later.

t. Review the recorded interview later on in order to analyze the data, prepare for future

Another great source for conducting interviews was produced by CHamoru ethnographer and oral historian, Rlene Santos Steffy and the CNMI Humanities Council, How to Conduct Oral History Interviews. This publication is free and accessible on-line: https://www.nmhcouncil.org/wp-content/uploads/HowToConductOralHistoryInterviews.pdf

Individual Genealogy Worksheet

INDIVIDUAL INFORMATION

Name   Date of Birth   Place of Birth

MATERNAL INFORMATION

Mother

Date of Birth & Place of Birth

Grandmother

Grandfather

Family Clan Names

PATERNAL INFORMATION

Father

Date of Birth & Place of Birth

Grandmother

Grandfather

Family Clan Names

SIBLING INFORMATION

SISTERS' NAMES

BROTHERS' NAMES

Notes about me and/or my family:

Family Group Worksheet

FAMILY GROUP WORKSHEET

Prepared by: _____   Date: _____

NAME:

	Date	Place
Birth		
Death		
Burial		

Father: Family Clan Name(s):
Mother: Family Clan Name(s):

SPOUSE:

	Date	Place
Birth		
Death		
Burial		

Father: Family Clan Name(s):
Mother: Family Clan Name(s):

Children	Female/Male	Date of Birth	Place of Birth
1			
2			
3			
4			
5			
6			
7			
8			

Ancestral Worksheet

Ancestral Worksheet

		2AA Great Grandmother
2A Grandmother	
		2AB Great Grandfather
2 Mother		2BA Great Grandmother
	2B Grandfather	
		2BB Great Grandfather
1 Name		3AA Great Grandmother
	3A Grandmother	
		3AB Great Grandfather
3 Father		3BA Great Grandmother
	3B Grandfather	
		3BB Great Grandfather

Written Release Form[50]

Written Release Form

Full Name of Person Interviewed

(print):_____

Address:_____

Phone: (   )_____

Place of
Interview:_____

Name of Interviewer & Institution
(print):_____

Date of Interview:_____

I understand that this interview and any photographs, tape recording, or video recording are part of scholarly research by the individual and institution named above. I give permission for the following (check all that apply):

_____May be used for educational and research purposes at the above
         institution
_____May include my name
_____May be included in a school publication or exhibit
_____May be included in another educational, nonprofit publication or exhibit
_____May be used but DO NOT include my name
_____May be deposited in a local, state or regional archive
_____Other (explain)

_____   _____
Signature of Interviewee   Date

_____   _____
Signature of Parent or Guardian if   Date
Interviewee Is a Minor

[50] Library of Congress, retrieved June 10, 2022, from:
https://www.loc.gov/folklife/edresources/edcenter_files/samplereleaseforms.pdf

Ancient Indigenous & CHamoru Words

Ancient Indigenous & CHamoru Words	English	Source
A'umachaguma'	Relations of the house, through connection, or some obligation	Freycinet (atugtcha-guma); Cunningham (a'umachaguma')
Achafñak	Blood relatives	Freycinet (atchafgnag)
Achakma'	Relations by friendship	Freycinet (atchagmak); Topping et.al. (achakma')
Adopta	Adopt	Pressig (adopta)
Åmko'	Old	Pressig (amco)
Apeyido	Surname; family name	Pressig (apeyido)
Apodo	Nickname	Hornbostel (apodo)
Asagua	Spouse	Pressig (asagua)
Atungo	Acquaintence	Pressig (atungo)
Biha/Biho	Old lady/man, sometmes referred to as grandmother/father	Pressig (bija/bijo)
Bisabuela'/Bisabuelo'	Great Grandmother/father	CHamoru.info
Bisañieta/Bisañieto	Great granddaughter/son	Pressig (bisnieta/bistnieto)
CHe'lu	Sibling	Freycinet (tchilu)
CHe'lu ya huyong	Cousin	Freycinet (tchilu dja hoyong)
Dibotsia/Yiniti	Divorce	Pressig (dibotsia, yiniti)
Fåmagu'on	Children	Pressig (famaguon)
Familia	Family	Pressig (familia)
Finañågo-hu	When a mother refers to a child she birthed.	Freycinet (finagnago ho)
Ganye	To adopt as one's own child	Pressig (Ganye)

Ancient Indigenous & CHamoru Words	English	Source
Guela'/Guelo'	Grandmother/Grandfather	Freycinet (guila); Pressig (guella, guello)
Håga	Daughter	Freycinet (haga); Pressig (jaga)
Håle'	Roots	Pressig (jäle)
Hoben	Young	Pressig (joben)
I solokña inatngånan	Refers to the younger sibling in relation to an older sibling	Freycinet (i sologguan inatnganan)
Iha/Iho	Daughter/Son	Pressig (ija/ijo)
Kuñåda/Kuñådo	Sister/Brother-in-law	Pressig (cuñada/cuñado)
Låhi	Son, man	Freycinet (lahi); Pressig (laji)
Måga/Magachaga	Refers to the eldest child in the family	Freycinet (maga, magatchaga)
Manggåfa	Family	Freycinet (manggafa)
Mayana na patgon	Abandoned child	Freycinet (madjna nga pagon)
Nåna	Mother	Freycinet (nana); Pressig (nana)
Neni	Baby	Pressig (nene)
Nenis	Only used when a father refers to his son or daughter.	Freycinet (ninis)
Nenis hegui	Refers to a daughter or son born out of wedlock	Freycinet (ninis hegui)
Nenis-hu	When a father refers to his child	Freycinet (ninis ho)
Ñieta/Ñieto	Granddaughter/son	Pressig (nieta/nieto)
Palao'an	Woman	Freycinet (pala-uan); Pressig (palauan)
Pårentes	Relatives	Pressig (parientes)
Påtgon	Child	Pressig (patgon)

Ancient Indigenous & CHamoru Words	English	Source
Pineksai	Refers to an adopted daughter/son	Freycinet (pinigsai); Pressig (pinegsai)
Poksai	To raise a child	Pressig (pogsai)
Prima/Primo	Cousin	Pressig (prima/primo)
Saina	Parents, ancestor, elder	Freycinet (saina); Pressig (saina)
Sobrina/Sobrino	Niece/nephew	Pressig (sobrina/sobrino)
Solokña	Refers to youngeet child in the family	Freycinet (sologgna)
Sotera/Sotero	Young unmarried female/male	Pressig (sottera/sottero)
Taotao	People, man	Pressig (taotao)
Tåta	Father	Pressig (tata)
Tiha/Tiho	Aunt/Uncle	Freycinet (tia); Pressig
Tronkon familia	Family lineage	Pressig (trongcon familia)
Yetna/Yetno	Daughter/Son-in-law	Pressig (yetna/yetno)

Glossary of Select Spanish Terms

In 1984 the Nieves M. Flores Memorial Library and the Micronesia Area Research worked in collaboration to fund and print Victor F. Mallada's, translation of the 1897 census conducted by the Spanish government. Mallada also included a glossary of Spanish words and abbreviations contained in the census. This glossary incorporates Mallada's and certain Spanish words that were used in the Guam Censo Official de 1920, a.k.a. 1920 Church Census, conducted by Father Roman Maria de Vera.

Spanish Words/Abbreviations	Definition
Abandono	Abandoned
Aga./Ago./ Agregra/Agrego	Agregada/Agregado: Any household other than sons and daughters
Altas	Increased membership
Bajas	Decreased membership
Ballenero	Whaling ship
Ca Po	Cura Parroco: Parish Priest
Ca/Co	Casada: Married woman | Casado: Married man
Caba / Cabs	Cabeceria: District | Cabecerias: Districts
Casas	Houses
Clases	Social Status. Sometimes indicates the type of family relationship, like in the case of household.
D/DA	Don/Doña: Title address equivalent to Mr./Mrs.
Descubierto	Newly registered adult
Difunta/Difunto	Deceased female/male
Divorciado	Divorced
Edades	Age
Esposa/esposo	Wife/Husband
Estados	Civil status

Spanish Words/Abbreviations	Definition
Gobernadllo	Gobernadorcillo: Commissioner
Hembras	Women
Hermana/Hermano	Sister / Brother
Hija/Hijo	Daughter/Son
hta	hasta: until
Huerfana/Huerfano	Orphan female/male
Madre / Padre	Mother / Father
Marido de	Husband of
Matrimonios	Marriages
ms	mes: month
Mtra/Mtro	Maestra/Maestro: Teacher
Muchacha/Muchacho	Girl/Boy
Mujor de	Wife of
Na/No	Nacida/Nacido: Born female/male
Nombres	Names
Pa/Po	Parvula/Parvulo: Child 7 years of age or younger female/male
Pariento (relative)	Relative
Prima/Primo	Cousin female/male
Pueblo	Town, generally in the rural areas.
Resumen	Summary
Rubrica	Signature. In brackets it indicates that the original is signed.
Sa/So	Soltera/Soltero: Single female/male
Separdo	Separated
Sobrina/Sobrino	Niece / Nephew
ut. infra / ut. supra	As described below/above
Va/Vo	Viuda/Viudo: Widow/Widower

Spanish Words/Abbreviations	Definition
Varones	Men
Visita	Village, settlement without a resident parish priest.
Vivo	Live
Vto. Bno/Vo Bo	Visto Bueno: Endorsed, Approved

Sample Ancestral Chart

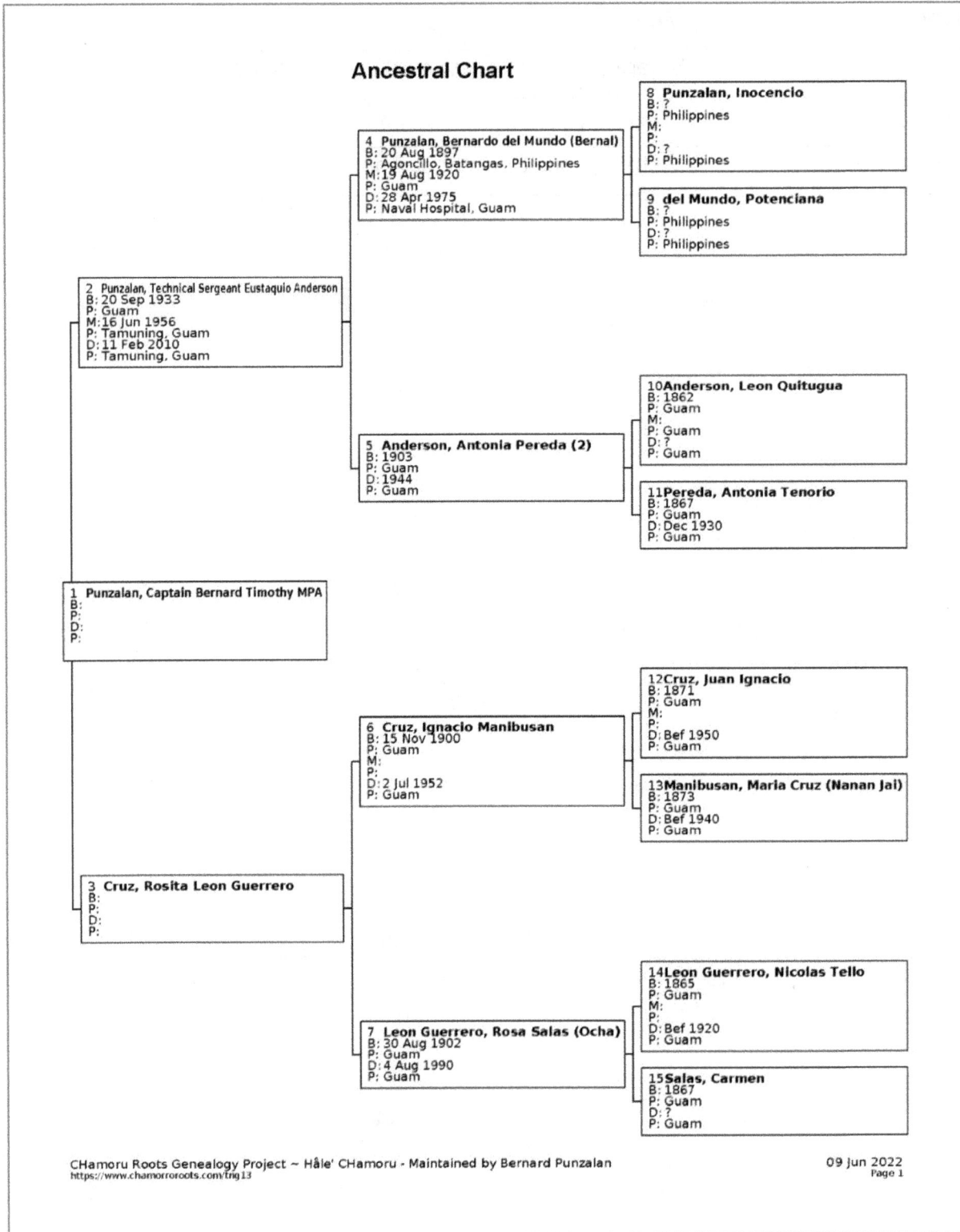

Ancestral Chart

8: Punzalan, Inocencio
B: ?
P: Philippines
M:
P:
D: ?
P: Philippines

4 Punzalan, Bernardo del Mundo (Bernal)
B: 20 Aug 1897
P: Agoncillo, Batangas, Philippines
M: 19 Aug 1920
P: Guam
D: 28 Apr 1975
P: Naval Hospital, Guam

9: del Mundo, Potenciana
B: ?
P: Philippines
D: ?
P: Philippines

2 Punzalan, Technical Sergeant Eustaquio Anderson
B: 20 Sep 1933
P: Guam
M: 16 Jun 1956
P: Tamuning, Guam
D: 11 Feb 2010
P: Tamuning, Guam

10 Anderson, Leon Quitugua
B: 1862
P: Guam
M:
P: Guam
D: ?
P: Guam

5 Anderson, Antonia Pereda (2)
B: 1903
P: Guam
D: 1944
P: Guam

11 Pereda, Antonia Tenorio
B: 1867
P: Guam
D: Dec 1930
P: Guam

1 Punzalan, Captain Bernard Timothy MPA
B:
P:
D:
P:

12 Cruz, Juan Ignacio
B: 1871
P: Guam
M:
P:
D: Bef 1950
P: Guam

6 Cruz, Ignacio Manibusan
B: 15 Nov 1900
P: Guam
M:
P:
D: 2 Jul 1952
P: Guam

13 Manibusan, Maria Cruz (Nanan Jai)
B: 1873
P: Guam
D: Bef 1940
P: Guam

3 Cruz, Rosita Leon Guerrero
B:
P:
D:
P:

14 Leon Guerrero, Nicolas Tello
B: 1865
P: Guam
M:
P:
D: Bef 1920
P: Guam

7 Leon Guerrero, Rosa Salas (Ocha)
B: 30 Aug 1902
P: Guam
D: 4 Aug 1990
P: Guam

15 Salas, Carmen
B: 1867
P: Guam
D: ?
P: Guam

Descendants of Bernardo del Mundo Punzalan

&

Antonia Pereda Anderson

©2022 Bernard T. Punzalan

Table of Contents

1

1a Bernardo del Mundo (Bernal) Punzalan*[1,2,3,4,5,6,7]

Birth:	20 Aug 1897, Agoncillo, Batangas, Philippines
Death:	28 Apr 1975, Naval Hospital, Guam
Burial:	May 1975, Pigo Cemetery, Anigua, Guam
Father:	Inocencio Punzalan[7] (? -?)
Mother:	Potenciana del Mundo[7] (? -?)
Clan:	Pansi

The Story of the Punzalan Clan on Guam
By: Bernard Punzalan

My grandfather ("Tata"), Bernardo del Mundo Punzalan, was from Agoncillo, Batangas Philippines. He was born on August 20, 1897. He is the youngest of seven siblings. He departed the Philippines with one of his brothers, Macario, sometime between 1916-1917 with a destination of San Francisco, California. Somehow, he made his way down to San Diego and joined the U.S. Navy around 1917.

Not long after his enlistment, he was stationed on Guam, where he eventually retired. On August 20, 1920 he married my grandmother Antonia Pereda Anderson (of Chamoru, Spanish, and Scottish descent), from Agana, Guam. Together they had a total of 11 children. In early 1944, Nana passed away. However, later that same year on November 15, 1944, Tata married Nana's sister, Engracia Pereda Anderson to help care for his children. It was not uncommon back then for a widow or widower to remarry the deceased spouse's sibling.

I have had a little less than five years to get to know Tata. The reason for this short period was because my Dad, Eustaquio, also known as "Pak," was in the Air Force. It was not until 1970 (when I was nine years old) when we returned to Guam and resettled for my Dad's retirement. On April 28, 1975 Tata lost his fight against cancer.

From what I do remember about Tata is that he was very kind and generous to us grandchildren. When we would visit him, he would usually give us candy, and if we were especially good, he would ask us if we were his "sugar babies," the name taken from one of the candies.

Tata's first house, from my recollection, was huge. It had three bedrooms, half a bathroom, a spacious living room, separate dining, separate kitchen, and an enclosed balcony-type patio. The wooden house was elevated about five feet above the ground. Under the house you would have found the outside shower, an area for Nina to wash and dry their clothes, a hammock to lay and relax (it was more for entertainment for us grandchildren who would use it to swing), and then there

2

were the chickens in the chicken coops. Oh yes, Tata raised chickens and was particularly attentive to his fighting roosters.

The house was situated on the Punzalan property on the Tiyan cliff line, marveling a fabulous view of the Ocean and the rest of Tamuning village. As you face the outside of his house to its front and if you look to the left, there use to be an outside Spanish type oven which was used for baking bread or "Pan Tosta", or even roasting chicken or pigs. My dad said that Tata built the oven sometime before World War II. The house and the chickens were later passed on to my Dad, after Tata moved into his concrete house. Today, there are no longer any remains of the wooden house or the Spanish oven. My house on Guam is situated partially where the oven and Tata's house was. However, Tata's concrete house is still in use and is the first house you will see as you enter the you enter the Punzalan properties.

Aside from Tata raising roosters and going to the cockfights, he was also a fisherman ("Talayero"). He manufactured his own fishing nets ("Talaya.") I can recall watching him sew his Talaya while smoking and gripping his Tiparillo cigar at the corner of his mouth. Amazingly the ashes from his cigar would just dangle and remain completely intact from the filter. It was an awesome sight to watch Tata working with diligence and patience while training his fighting cocks and sewing his talaya.

Tata spoke at least three languages: Tagalog, English and Chamoru. He was approximately five feet one inch tall and weighed about 105 lbs. His death was the first of the family I have ever experienced since we came back to Guam...making it the most traumatic for me. As I grew older I use to think that Tata's death was the end to ever knowing the rest of the Punzalan Clan. That thought has now perished.

Through the assistance of my father's friends and the Philippine Consulate on Guam we were able to establish contact with our family in the Philippines around 1996.   In May 1997, my father, mother, one of my sons and I visited with our family and attended my cousin Resty Punzalan's wedding in Taal. We also visited with Uncle Jess and his family in Ayala Alabang. This visit and several others finally led to a historic Punzalan Grand Reunion in 2000 between some of the Punzalan Clan on Guam and Punzalan Clan in the Philippines. I know we are long overdue for another Reunion and look forward to the day where we can meet again.

Spouse:	Antonia Pereda (2) Anderson[8,3,1,2,5,6,7] (1903-1944)
Birth:	1903, Guam
Burial:	1944, Pigo Cemetery, Anigua, Guam
Death:	1944, Guam
Father:	Leon Quitugua Anderson[8,9,10,7] (1862-?)

3

Mother: **Antonia Tenorio Pereda**[8,11,12,13,7] (1867-Dec 1930)

Clan: Che

Marriage: 19 Aug 1920, Guam[1]

11 Children...

    Donato Anderson (30 Apr 1921-20 Aug 1924)

    Antonio Anderson (28 Nov 1922-5 Jan 1997)

    Jesus Anderson (27 Jun 1924-30 Jun 1924)

    Jose Isaac Anderson (3 Jun 1925-1 Mar 2001)

    Nieves Anderson (Bing) (5 Aug 1927-5 Aug 2009)

    Emilia Anderson (Bilang) (30 Jun 1929-21 Jun 2008)

    Victoria Anderson (Dola) (7 May 1931-20 May 1990)

    Technical Sergeant Eustaquio Anderson (20 Sep 1933-11 Feb 2010)

    Lourdes Anderson (Lutdes) (14 Feb 1936-)

    Felicita Anderson (Cid) (1937-)

    Josefina Anderson (Minang) (10 Apr 1940-16 Sep 2010)

Other spouses: Engracia Pereda Anderson

1a.1 Donato Anderson Punzalan[2,7]

Birth: 30 Apr 1921, Guam[2]

Death: 20 Aug 1924

Father: **Bernardo del Mundo (Bernal) Punzalan**[1,2,3,4,5,6,7] (20 Aug 1897-28 Apr 1975)

Mother: **Antonia Pereda (2) Anderson**[8,3,1,2,5,6,7] (1903-1944)

1a.2 Antonio Anderson Punzalan[5,7]

Birth: 28 Nov 1922, Guam

Burial: 13 Jan 1997, Pigo Cemetery, Anigua, Guam

Death: 5 Jan 1997, Guam

Father: **Bernardo del Mundo (Bernal) Punzalan**[1,2,3,4,5,6,7] (20 Aug 1897-28 Apr 1975)

Mother: **Antonia Pereda (2) Anderson**[8,3,1,2,5,6,7] (1903-1944)

Spouse: **Ana Rojas Sablan**[14,7] (10 Feb 1921-3 Jun 2011)

Birth: 10 Feb 1921, Guam[14]

Death: 3 Jun 2011, Guam

Burial: 14 Jun 2011, Pigo Catholic Cemetery, Anigua, Guam

Father: **Joaquin Delgado Sablan**[15,16,17,18,19,14,20,21,7] (4 Nov 1887-1 Nov 1968)

Mother: **Amalia Atoigue Rojas**[22,23,18,19,14,20,24,21,7] (18 Nov 1890-6 Jun 1972)

Clan: Dong / Dongat

4

Sample Book Report from Reunion family tree software.

2 Children...

1a.3 Jesus Anderson Punzalan[20,20,7]

Birth:	27 Jun 1924, Guam[20]
Death:	30 Jun 1924, Guam[20]
Father:	**Bernardo del Mundo (Bernal) Punzalan**[1,2,3,4,5,6,7] (20 Aug 1897-28 Apr 1975)
Mother:	**Antonia Pereda (2) Anderson**[8,3,1,2,5,6,7] (1903-1944)

1a.4 Jose Isaac Anderson Punzalan[5,25,7]

Birth:	3 Jun 1925, Agana, Guam
Death:	1 Mar 2001, Guam
Burial:	Guam Veteran's Cemetery, Piti, Guam
Father:	**Bernardo del Mundo (Bernal) Punzalan**[1,2,3,4,5,6,7] (20 Aug 1897-28 Apr 1975)
Mother:	**Antonia Pereda (2) Anderson**[8,3,1,2,5,6,7] (1903-1944)
Spouse:	**Sylvia Iglesias San Nicolas**[26,7] (3 Nov 1927-)
Birth:	3 Nov 1927, Agana, Guam
Father:	**Francisco Guerrero San Nicolas**[27,26,7] (1899-?)
Mother:	**Joaquina Guerrero Iglesias**[28,27,26,29,7] (1899-20 Apr 1984)
Marriage:	9 Jul 1949, Tamuning, Guam

10 Children...

1a.5 Nieves Anderson (Bing) Punzalan[5,7]

Birth:	5 Aug 1927, Guam
Death:	5 Aug 2009, San Diego, California

5

Sample Book Report from Reunion family tree software.

Father: **Bernardo del Mundo (Bernal) Punzalan**[1,2,3,4,5,6,7] (20 Aug 1897-28 Apr 1975)

Mother: **Antonia Pereda (2) Anderson**[8,3,1,2,5,6,7] (1903-1944)

Nieves Anderson Punzalan Tongco
Published in the San Diego Union-Tribune on 8/30/2009

TONGCO, NIEVES "BING" Nieves "Bing" Tongco was born in Guam on August 5, 1927. She grew up amidst World War II and raised her younger siblings (who adorned her with the nickname "Bing"). On January 19, 1947, Bing married Jose Tongco. They settled in San Diego and their home became a focal point for family gatherings. It was a common sight to see a big group enjoying her home-cooked food. Bing had a knack with games particularly mah jong and cards. While playing she would tell stories of the internment camp in Guam, and various tales about her family. She had a generous heart and fierce spirit. Bing would do anything for a loved one and her care was far-reaching. She truly enjoyed being around children. She worked as a teacher's assistant and the kids knew the love of a grandmother under her care. Bing instinctively redefined the word family to suit her vast ability to love. Many people genuinely called her family without needing the claim of blood ties. Bing died peacefully on August 5, 2009, surrounded by family and loved ones. Bing is survived by one brother, three sisters, six children, sixteen grandchildren and five great-grandchildren.

Spouse: **Jose Castro Tongco**[7] (28 Aug 1920-22 Jun 1989)
Birth: 28 Aug 1920, Philippines
Death: 22 Jun 1989, San Diego, California
Marriage: 19 Jan 1947, Guam

6 Children...

1a.6 Emilia Anderson (Bilang) Punzalan[30,5,7]

Birth: 30 Jun 1929, Guam
Death: 21 Jun 2008, Barrigada, Guam
Father: **Bernardo del Mundo (Bernal) Punzalan**[1,2,3,4,5,6,7] (20 Aug 1897-28 Apr 1975)
Mother: **Antonia Pereda (2) Anderson**[8,3,1,2,5,6,7] (1903-1944)

Spouse: **Galo Garrido San Nicolas**[31,30,7] (8 Oct 1932-5 Feb 1997)
Birth: 8 Oct 1932, Guam

6

Death: 5 Feb 1997, Lathrop, California
Father: **Enrique Rosario San Nicolas**[20,32,33,34,7] (1904-?)
Mother: **Ana Mendiola Garrido**[35,20,36,33,37,7] (1905-bef 1940)
Clan: Camudu

6 Children...

1a.7 Victoria Anderson (Dola) Punzalan[5,21,6,7]

Birth: 7 May 1931, Guam
Death: 20 May 1990, Los Angeles, California
Burial: 28 May 1990, Pigo Cemetery, Anigua, Guam
Father: **Bernardo del Mundo (Bernal) Punzalan**[1,2,3,4,5,6,7] (20 Aug 1897-28 Apr 1975)
Mother: **Antonia Pereda (2) Anderson**[8,3,1,2,5,6,7] (1903-1944)

Spouse: **Juan Santos Gogue**[21,6,7] (1 Feb 1931-25 Apr 1979)
Birth: 1 Feb 1931, Guam
Burial: 5 May 1979, Pigo Cemetery, Anigua, Guam
Death: 25 Apr 1979, Guam
Father: **Agustin San Luis Gogue**[38,39,40,41,42,43,6,7] (abt 1895-?)
Mother: **Antonia Santos Santos**[44,38,39,40,41,45,42,43,6,7] (1895-?)
Clan: Bita / Sohgue

10 Children...

Sample Book Report from Reunion family tree software.

7

1a.8 Technical Sergeant Eustaquio Anderson Punzalan[5,7]

Birth:	20 Sep 1933, Guam
Death:	11 Feb 2010, Tamuning, Guam
Burial:	19 Feb 2010, Guam Veteran's Cemetery, Piti, Guam
Father:	**Bernardo del Mundo (Bernal) Punzalan**[1,2,3,4,5,6,7] (20 Aug 1897-28 Apr 1975)
Mother:	**Antonia Pereda (2) Anderson**[8,3,1,2,5,6,7] (1903-1944)
Clan:	Pansi / Che'

Eustaquio Anderson Punzalan
Funeral Announcement
Published in Pacific Daily News from February 16 to March 16, 2010

Pak - USAF Retired - Born September 20, 1933, was called to his eternal rest on February 11, 2010. Last Respects for will be held on Friday, February 19th beginning at 9 a.m. and concluding at 12:30 p.m. at Saint Anthony Catholic Church in Tamuning. Mass for a Christian burial will be offered at 1 p.m. Interment will follow at Guam Veterans Cemetery in Piti, where we will bid him farewell and a peaceful rest.

-

Honoring My Father and Four Generations of US Military Service
Bernard Punzalan, March 27, 2014

Although some of this is anecdotal and primarily from my personal talks with my father, Eustaquio Anderson Punzalan (deceased), a retired U.S. Air Force veteran, and others who I have observed talked with, some of these Veterans of World War II, Korean War, Vietnam War do not talk much about the combat experiences because when they became a part of the military they understood the potential consequences and sacrifices they would have to make. They understood the value of patriotism towards duty, honor and country. For them, it was not so much about the benefits and opportunity, but a sense of duty and a way of serving and being able to contribute back to the community for the ideals and appreciation for what they were taught to believe.

From one of my personal communications with Mr. Candido Taitano San Agustin (deceased), he and my father along with several other Chamorro men enlisted in the Air Force and had their basic training on Guam in the early 1950's. According to Mr. San Agustin, after their basic training the Air Force wasn't quite sure yet what to do with these newly acquired citizen-recruits so they remained serving on Guam. Eventually, things got sorted out and these men were assigned worldwide. It is not too difficult to imagine their sense of duty and patriotism after experiencing first-hand the Japanese occupation of Guam from World War II was still quite fresh.

8

As a child, I recall hearing about his Air Base being attacked during one of his two tours in Vietnam; however, not once did he ever want to talk about it or any other combative engagement he may have faced. His choice of memories that he shared with me were limited to positive ones. Stories like how the Chamorro people in the military would rally together, network and take care of each other in collocated assignments whether in a war zone or in a peaceful assignment. No matter where he was assigned there was Chamorro camaraderie.

Some of his assignments during his military career took him to Korea, Montana, Wyoming, California (several assignments), Vietnam, Okinawa, Spain and with a final assignment back home on Guam for his retirement in 1972. Many of these assignments included our family accompanying him. It was not an easy task for him and my mother (Rosita Leon Guerrero Cruz) to relocate and take care of seven children (at the time, the eighth child came after his retirement). On several occasions I recall it was my mother having to relocate us, while my father left in advance of us to find and settle our housing arrangements before we arrived.

When my father was alive, he did not press forward to apply for and receive any type of Veteran benefits. He did not feel right to claim for additional benefits when he knew that there were others more deserving and in need of those entitlements for having sacrificed more in direct combat. My father was a very humble man. A man of honor and quite firm and final with his decisions once he made them. It was not until his final few years of life when our family was able to convince him to apply for the Veteran's benefits for which he was eligible.

My father's military service is preceded by his father's, Bernardo del Mundo Punzalan, a Filipino who served and retired with the U.S. Navy and settled on Guam since 1917. My father was also succeeded by my brother David Punzalan and me both U.S. Army, and my sister Noreen Punzalan San Agustin, U.S. Air Force. Our family's military service is now in its fourth generation of service: Paul Guerrero, Brandon Punzalan, Bryant Punzalan, Trevor Cruz, Nathan Punzalan and Andre San Agustin have all followed and honored their grandfather's footsteps serving in the U.S. Air Force.

Spouse: Rosita Leon Guerrero Cruz[46,7] (22 Aug 1937-)
Birth: 22 Aug 1937, Guam
Father: Ignacio Manibusan Cruz[47,48,46,7] (15 Nov 1900-2 Jul 1952)
Mother: Rosa Salas (Ocha) Leon Guerrero[49,48,46,7] (30 Aug 1902-4 Aug 1990)
Clan: Jai / Mafongfong / Matias
Marriage: 16 Jun 1956, Tamuning, Guam

8 Children...

1a.9 Lourdes Anderson (Lutdes) Punzalan[5,7]

Birth:	14 Feb 1936, Guam
Father:	**Bernardo del Mundo (Bernal) Punzalan**[1,2,3,4,5,6,7] (20 Aug 1897-28 Apr 1975)
Mother:	**Antonia Pereda (2) Anderson**[8,3,1,2,5,6,7] (1903-1944)
Spouse:	**Jose Martinez (Peling/Joe) Flores**[7,50] (17 Mar 1932-12 Mar 2014)
Birth:	17 Mar 1932, Guam[51]
Death:	12 Mar 2014, Guam
Burial:	22 Mar 2014, Guam Memorial Park Cemetery, Leyang, Barrigada, Guam
Father:	**Benigno Leon Guerrero Flores**[52,51,53,7] (1910-29 Nov 1999)
Mother:	**Dolores Matanane Martinez**[51,53,7] (1913-?)
Clan:	Apu / Bing
Divorce:	1977, Guam

7 Children...

1a.10 Felicita Anderson (Cid) Punzalan[54,7]

Birth:	1937, Guam
Father:	**Bernardo del Mundo (Bernal) Punzalan**[1,2,3,4,5,6,7] (20 Aug 1897-28 Apr 1975)
Mother:	**Antonia Pereda (2) Anderson**[8,3,1,2,5,6,7] (1903-1944)
Spouse:	**Phillip Siana**[7]

1 Child...

10

1a.11 Josefina Anderson (Minang) Punzalan[55,7]

Birth:	10 Apr 1940, Guam
Death:	16 Sep 2010, Leesville, Louisiana
Burial:	27 Sep 2010, Forest Lawn Cemetery, Leesville, Louisiana
Father:	**Bernardo del Mundo (Bernal) Punzalan**[1,2,3,4,5,6,7] (20 Aug 1897-28 Apr 1975)
Mother:	**Antonia Pereda (2) Anderson**[8,3,1,2,5,6,7] (1903-1944)

Josefina Punzalan Cruz was born in Hagata, Guam on April 10, 1940. A resident of Leesville, Louisiana for 20 years, passed away at Byrd Regional Hospital on September 16, 2010. She is predeceased by her husband Jesus Cruz; son Marcus Cruz; parents, Bernardo & Antonia Anderson Punzalan; brothers, Antonio, Jose & Eustaquio Punzalan and sisters, Nieves, Emilia & Victoria. Her kindness and generosity will live in the hearts of sisters, Lourdes Flores & Felicita Siana; her grandson Ryan Cruz; adopted sister, Lucy Blas and numerous nieces, nephews, cousins, godchildren and friends. Visitation will be held from 5 pm - 9 pm, Sunday, September 26, 2010 at the funeral home, with a rosary being recited at 6:00 pm. Funeral services for Josefina Punzalan Cruz, 70, of Leesville, Louisiana will be held at 1:00 p.m. Monday, September 27, 2010 at St. Michael the Archangel Catholic Church in Leesville with the Father Kenneth Michiels officiating. Burial will follow in the Forest Lawn Cemetery in Leesville, LA under the direction of Labby Memorial Funeral Home of Leesville.

Spouse:	**Jesus Esteban Cruz**[55,7] (3 Jun 1942-11 Nov 2003)
Birth:	3 Jun 1942, Guam
Death:	11 Nov 2003, Fort Polk, Louisiana
Burial:	Forest Lawn Cemetery, Leesville, Louisiana
Father:	**Miguel Cruz**[7] (? -?)
Mother:	**Carmen Eclavea Esteban**[7] (19 Nov 1914-?)
Clan:	Mabong

Jesus Esteban Cruz

Mr. Cruz died Tuesday, Nov. 11, in the Bayne-Jones Army Community Hospital in Fort Polk.

He was born in Dededo, Guam and a veteran of 22 years in the U.S. Army. He retired as a first sergeant. He was employed with Cubic at Fort Polk. He lived in Leesville since 1983 and was a member of the St. Michael's Catholic Church, Knights of Columbus Council #4156, Veterans of Foreign Wars, American Legion Post #145 in Leesville and was a veteran of the Vietnam War.

Survivors include his wife, Josefina Cruz of Leesville; two brothers, Peter Cruz of Waynesville, Mo., and Joseph Cruz of Alabama; three sisters, Carmen Santos, Margaret Cochran and Florentina Cruz, all of California, and one grandchild.

Funeral services for Mr. Jesus Esteban Cruz, 60, of Leesville will be
held at 10 a.m. Wednesday, Nov. 19, in the St. Michael's Catholic
Church in Leesville with Father Angelo Messina officiating. Burial will
follow in the Forest Lawn Cemetery in Leesville under the direction of
the Labby Memorial Funeral Home of Leesville. Mr. Cruz died Tuesday,
Nov. 11, in the Bayne-Jones Army Community Hospital in Fort Polk.
He was born in Dededo, Quam and a veteran of 22 years in the U.S.
Army and was a veteran of the Vietnam War. Survivors include his
wife, Josefina Cruz of Leesville; two brothers, Peter Cruz of
Waynesville, Mo., and Joseph Cruz of Alabama; three sisters,
Carmen Santos, Margaret Cochran and Florentina Cruz, all of
California, and one grandchild.

U.S. Veterans Gravesites, ca. 1775-2006
Name:
Jesus Esteban Cruz
Service Info.:
1SG US ARMY VIETNAM
Birth Date:
3 Jun 1942
Death Date:
11 Nov 2003
Cemetery:
Forest Lawn Cemetery
Cemetery Address:
400 S 6th Street Leesville, LA 71446

1 Child...

1b Bernardo del Mundo (Bernal) Punzalan (See above)

Spouse: **Engracia Pereda Anderson**[8,56,7] (12 Apr 1899-10 Oct 1988)
Birth: 12 Apr 1899, Guam
Death: 10 Oct 1988, Guam
Burial: 15 Oct 1988, Pigo Cemetery, Anigua, Guam

12

Sample Book Report from Reunion family tree software.

Father: **Leon Quitugua Anderson**[8,9,10,7] (1862-?)
Mother: **Antonia Tenorio Pereda**[8,11,12,13,7] (1867-Dec 1930)
Marriage: 15 Nov 1944, Aporguan, Dededo, Guam

Other spouses: Antonia Pereda (2) Anderson

Sample Book Report from Reunion family tree software.

13

Sources

1. "Guam News Letter." September 1920.
2. Ibid. May 1921.
3. "The Guam Recorder." August 1920.
4. "1930 U.S. Federal Census, Island of Guam." District 13, Naval Reservations and Ships, Radio, Sheet 16B.
5. "1940 U.S. Federal Census, Island of Guam." District 1-5, Agana, Barrio of Padre Palomo, Sheet 6B.
6. Jaryna Anjelique Gogue Balbas, "Personal communications to Bernard Punzalan," www.chamorroroots.com, 15 June 2020.
7. Bernard T. Punzalan, "CHamorro Roots Genealogy Project | http://www.chamorroroots.com," http://www.chamorroroots.com, "CHamorro Roots Genealogy Project (www.chamorroroots.com)," @R00007@, http://www.chamorroroots.com. Source Medium: Internet
8. Father Roman Maria de Vera, M.C., 19 May 1921, "Censo Oficial de 1920 (1920 Church Census)," Page 95.
9. Paul B. Souder, "Familian Chamorro: A Genealogy of Resident Families on Guam During the 19th and 20 Centuries," 1981, pg. 34 - Leon Quitugua Anderson (b1870); page 367.
10. "1920 U.S. Federal Census, Island of Guam." District 2, Agana City, Soledad Street, Sheet 11A.
11. "The Guam Recorder." January 1931.
12. Paul B. Souder, "Familian Chamorro: A Genealogy of Resident Families on Guam During the 19th and 20 Centuries," 1981, page 34 - Antonia Tenorio Pereda; page 367.
13. "1897 Census of the Mariana Islands," @R00002@, Micronesian Area Research Center, Mangilao, Guam, District 2, Agana City, Soledad Street, Sheet 11A.
14. "Guam News Letter." March 1921.
15. Mari Martinez Hernandez, "Vicente Guzman Sablan & Vicenta Borja Delgado," 23, 2010, Mari Martinez Hernandez.
16. "Familian Chamorro Genealogy Database Index: Patron de Almas: Ano de 1897 [Census]," Micronesian Area Research Center, Mangilao, Guam, Cabeceria No. 20 Pg. 99-86a; Age: 11. Source Medium: Internet
17. "1920 U.S. Federal Census, Island of Guam." District 1, Yigo Road, Sheet 53A/53B, 1920 U.S. Federal Census, Island of Guam.
18. "Guam News Letter." January 1917, Guam News Letter.
19. Ibid. December 1918.
20. "The Guam Recorder." August 1924.
21. Frankie Aguigui Farfan, "Email to Bernard Punzalan," CHamorro Roots Genealogy Project | www.CHamorroRoots.com, 21 Jan 2013.
22. "FamilySearch.org."

Source Medium: Internet AMALIA CASTRO ROJAS, b.1890, Guam   Compact Disc #123   Pin #26535, 3.

23. "1897 Census of the Mariana Islands," @R00002@, Micronesian Area Research Center, Mangilao, Guam, Cabeceria No. 8a. Pg. 99-34a. Age 7. There may have another Amalia Atoigue Rojas.

24. "Guam Pacific Daily News Funeral & Obituaries." Jun 1972.

25. "Listing of Deaths," Memorandum, Office of Vital Statistics, Department of Public Health, Government of Guam, 9 Apr 2001.

26. "1940 U.S. Federal Census, Island of Guam." District 1-5, Municipality of Agana, Padre Palomo Barrio, Sheet 12B.

27. "Guam News Letter." March 1922.

28. "1920 U.S. Federal Census, Island of Guam." District 1, Agana City, De La Corte Street, Sheet 26A.

29. "Guam Pacific Daily News Funeral & Obituaries." Apr 1984.

30. "Corena Sanchez email to Bernard Punzalan," Chamorro Roots Genealogy Project | www.ChamorroRoots.com, 2 Nov 2011.

31. "1940 U.S. Federal Census, Island of Guam." District 1-8, Municipality of Agana, Agana City, Sheet 2A.

32. "1920 U.S. Federal Census, Island of Guam." District 2, Agana City, San Juan de Letran Street, Sheet 52B.

33. "1930 U.S. Federal Census, Island of Guam." District 1, Agana City, Isabel la Catolica Street, Sheet 19A.

34. "1940 U.S. Federal Census, Island of Guam." District 1-9, Agana, Agana City, Sheet 23A.

35. "Henry Garrido email to Bernard Punzalan."
Source Medium: Electronic 19 Sep 08.

36. "1920 U.S. Federal Census, Island of Guam." District 2, Agana City, Santa Cruz Street, Sheet 43A.

37. Roman Maria de Vera, M.C., 1920, "Censo Oficial de 1920 Guam (transcribed by author). Archivo de lost Padres Capuchinos, Burlada, Navarra, Spain.," Page 17.

38. "Guam News Letter." September 1916.

39. Ibid. October 1915.

40. Ibid. January 1918.

41. Ibid. December 1919.

42. Ibid. December 1921.

43. "The Guam Recorder." February 1924.

44. "1897 Census of the Mariana Islands," @R00002@, Micronesian Area Research Center, Mangilao, Guam, Cabeceria No. 12a. Pg. 99-49a.

15

Sample Book Report from Reunion family tree software.

45. "1920 U.S. Federal Census, Island of Guam." District 1, Agana City, Castillo Street, Sheet 54A.

46. "1940 U.S. Federal Census, Island of Guam." District 1-4, Agana, Agana City, Sheet 25A.

47. Roman Maria de Vera, M.C., 1920, "Censo Oficial de 1920 Guam (transcribed by author). Archivo de lost Padres Capuchinos, Burlada, Navarra, Spain.," Page 20.

48. "1930 U.S. Federal Census, Island of Guam." District 3, Agana, Bilibic Agana Urban, Soledad Street, Sheet 6A.

49. "1920 U.S. Federal Census, Island of Guam." District 1, Agana City, Isabel la Catolica Street, Sheet 38B, 1920 U.S. Federal Census. (District 1, Agana City, Isabel la Catolica, Street, Sheet 38B).

50. "Guam Pacific Daily News Funeral & Obituaries." 20 Mar 2014.

51. "The Guam Recorder." May 1932.

52. "1920 U.S. Federal Census, Island of Guam." District 1, Agana City, La Corte Street, Sheet 26A.

53. "The Guam Recorder." November 1937.

54. "1940 U.S. Federal Census, Island of Guam." District 1-5, Agana, Barrio of Padre Palomo, Sheet 6B. Listed as Teresita.

55. "Private email to Bernard Punzalan," CHamorro Roots Genealogy Project: www.CHamorroRoots.com, 22 Jun 2011.

56. "1930 U.S. Federal Census, Island of Guam." District 3, Agana, Bilibic Agana Urban, Soledad Street, Sheet 8A.

Sample Book Report from Reunion family tree software.

Sample Book Report from Reunion family tree software.

17

www.ingramcontent.com/pod-product-compliance
Lightning Source LLC
Chambersburg PA
CBHW080255030426
42334CB00023BA/2822